simply
beautiful

beading

53 QUICK AND
EASY PROJECTS

heidi boyd

David & Charles

A DAVID & CHARLES BOOK
David & Charles is a subsidiary of F+W (UK) Ltd.,
an F+W Publications Inc. company

First published in the UK in 2004
First published in the USA by North Light,
an imprint of F+W Publications Ltd, in 2004
First reprint 2005
Second reprint 2006
Third reprint 2008
Copyright © Heidi Boyd 2004

ISBN 13: 978 0 7153 1880 5
ISBN 10: 0 7153 1880 2

Printed in China by SNP-Leefung
for David & Charles
Brunel House   Newton Abbot   Devon

Visit our website at www.davidandcharles.co.uk

David & Charles books are available from all
good bookshops; alternatively you can contact
our Orderline on (0)1626 334555 or write to us at
FREEPOST EX2 110, David & Charles Direct, Newton
Abbot, TQ12 4ZZ (no stamp required UK mainland).

Editor: Jolie Lamping Roth
Designer: Stephanie Strang
Layout Artist: Donna Cozatchy
Production Coordinator: Sara Dumford
Photographers: Christine Polomsky, Tim Grondin,
Al Parrish and Hal Barkin
Photo Stylist: Jan Nickum and Nora Martini

metric conversion chart

TO CONVERT	TO	MULTIPLY BY
Inches	Centimetres	2.54
Centimetres	Inches	0.4
Feet	Centimetres	30.5
Centimetres	Feet	0.03
Yards	Metres	0.9
Metres	Yards	1.1
Sq. Inches	Sq. Centimetres	6.45
Sq. Centimetres	Sq. Inches	0.16
Sq. Feet	Sq. Metres	0.09
Sq. Metres	Sq. Feet	10.8
Sq. Yards	Sq. Metres	0.8
Sq. Metres	Sq. Yards	1.2
Pounds	Kilograms	0.45
Kilograms	Pounds	2.2
Ounces	Grams	28.4
Grams	Ounces	0.04

ABOUT THE
author

Artist **HEIDI BOYD** creates innovative craft projects for both children and adults, emphasizing the elements of surprise and accessibility. In addition to **SIMPLY BEAUTIFUL BEADING**, Heidi has authored **WIZARD CRAFTS**, **PET CRAFTS** and **FAIRY CRAFTS**, all published by North Light Books. She's contributed proprietary projects to **BETTER HOMES AND GARDENS** magazines and craft books.

With a degree in fine arts, Heidi has taught workshops and art classes in schools and art centers for over a decade. She lives in Maine with her husband, two sons and dog.

DEDICATED TO…

Tricia Waddell, Peggy Leonardo, Barb Palar and Nancy Wyatt, creative women who've opened doors and placed their trust in me; Yvonne Naanep, who is always there to share ideas with; my sister, Sasha, because I love you; my mum, Karina, who bought my very first beads and then later vacuumed half of them back up off the floor (if you only knew what you'd started); my wonderful boys, Jasper and Elliot, who're both relieved their bead-shopping days are behind them; and most especially Jon, without whose love and support this book would never have been written.

acknowledgments · This book was born through the hard work of many and never could have been realized alone. I'd like to extend thanks to my wonderful editor, Jolie Lamping Roth, who successfully squeezed all the projects into this book, and then painstakingly edited through them. Also to Christine Polomsky, who good-naturedly survived the nonstop ordeal of photographing each and every step. And to Stephanie Strang, whose graphic design talents made this book Simply Beautiful!

contents

introduction

have you ever stood in a store holding a package of irresistible beads, knowing that you wanted to buy them but having no idea what you would do with them? I've found myself in the very same position, bewildered by the endless varieties of beads and unsure what I would create with them. Until I was given the opportunity to write this book, I'd looked longingly at the beads but never committed the time or energy to fully explore the creative possibilities they held.

As a child I'd been content to bead daisy chains of seed beads on fishing line. In the many years since, the selection of jewelry-making supplies has exploded. Free to invest all my time and energy into beading, I filled my basket with the beads I'd been resisting. I'd landed in the candy store of my childhood dreams. I returned to my studio with bags of beads and the latest gear, inspired to tackle my mission: to design beautiful beaded jewelry and accessories that are quick and easy to make.

Before long, errant beads were rolling underfoot, and I had fully grasped the enormity of my task. I wanted to create jewelry in a range of styles using a vast variety of beads in the hopes of inspiring beaders of all ages. After countless hours experimenting with different techniques and materials, I chose only the simplest, most successful techniques to place in this book. In the process, I also sorted through the myriad of jewelry-making equipment and narrowed it down to a few essential elements.

It took many more trips back to craft and bead stores, but in the end I've filled this book with over fifty-three projects and variations that I guarantee you'll love to make, wear and give. So, next time you find yourself holding gorgeous beads, don't hesitate; just buy them. I assure you you'll find in the following pages a "Simply Beautiful" way to use them.

Heidi

beads

It's an understatement to say there is a wide variety of beads on the market. Although I have tried to incorporate many different varieties in this book, I've only managed to scratch the surface of what's available. Each time I went shopping I found a new bead type that inspired yet another project design. At some point I had to stop; I could have only so many pages in the book. The following is a brief introduction of the different varieties of beads featured in the projects. Please keep in mind that the following photographs are only a sampling; while shopping you'll find color, finish and size variations within each bead type.

bead types

| **SEED BEADS** | The smallest beads used in this book, glass seed beads are inexpensive and come in a wide range of colors. There are variations in the openings and sizes of these beads; make sure the ones you select work with the specified needles, beading cord or thread. If you like uniformity and a wider opening choose the more expensive Delica brand of seed beads. | **"E" BEADS** | Larger than seed beads, "E" beads also have inherent color and size variations. Faster to string, "E" beads are useful for framing and spacing other beads. | **BUGLES** | Bugle beads are small tubes of glass that come in different lengths and colors. Their openings are close in size to those of seed beads. The shorter the bugle bead, the more light the finished piece will reflect; but the longer the bugle, the faster the strand will string together. | **PRESSED GLASS** | These glass beads have been

stamped into specific shapes. The most common forms are leaves, flowers and stars, although you can sometimes find animals and fruits. | **CRYSTALS** | Faceted crystal beads reflect light and add sparkle to any beaded piece. They come in round, cube and bicone shapes. The prices of these beads vary dramatically; the more-expensive Austrian varieties such as Swarovski lead crystal are clearer and more reflective than the less-expensive generic crystal beads. | **GLASS PEARLS** | These imitation pearls are glass beads that are covered with a pearlescent coating. They are an affordable and effective costume jewelry alternative to natural pearls.

| **CERAMIC** | Ceramic beads are made with clay that has been kiln fired, painted with a glaze, and then fired a second time to bring out the sheen in the finish and protect the clay.

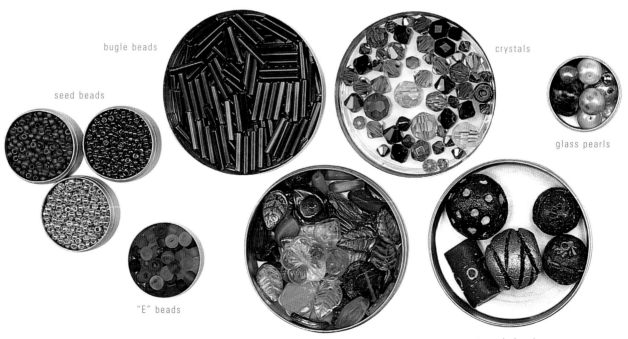

bugle beads

seed beads

crystals

glass pearls

"E" beads

pressed glass beads

ceramic beads

| SILVER OR METAL-PLATED BEADS | These accurately sized beads range in price from inexpensive metal-finished beads to more-expensive sterling silver beads. They are good simple spacer beads to place between ornate beads. | RHINESTONES | Small rhinestones are set in metal disks, heart shapes or round bead shapes. These accent beads add sparkle and interest to a piece. | SPACERS | Metal-finished spacer beads come in a variety of shapes and sizes. Keep a selection on hand, as their neutral color makes them the perfect accompaniment to almost all bead types. | POLYMER CLAY BEADS | Polymer clay beads (not shown below) are made with colored synthetic clay that is hardened in an oven. The clay comes in bright colors that create vibrant beads. You can easily make your own beads or purchase manufactured varieties. | ART GLASS | These vibrant handcrafted glass beads are decorated with spots and swirls of contrasting colored glass. | FURNACE GLASS | Canes of glass are fused together and then sliced to make modern beads with stripes of color. | MILLEFIORI (OR MULTICHIP) BEADS | Millefiori beads (not shown below) have brilliant colored flowers or designs that are created with small, brightly colored glass canes. The design is usually framed by contrasting dark-colored glass. | SHELLS | Common shells are transformed into beads by being drilled from top to bottom or down the middle. Expect natural variations in the sizes, colors and shapes of these beads.

| MIRACLE BEADS | These round beads have a luminous metallic finish that captures the light. Always perfectly round, they come in a variety of colors from vibrant to subtle. | AFRICAN CHRISTMAS BEADS | These are an imported mixture of glass beads in a variety of shapes and colors. If you have trouble locating them, combine striped "E" beads along with assorted tube and round colored glass beads.

FIRST-TIME BEADERS

If you're just getting started with beading, consider purchasing variety packs along with neutral-colored seed beads, "E" beads and metal spacer beads. A stock of neutral beads will help fill in between the more-expensive beads. Buying beads one at a time is helpful if you're working on a specific design, but it's more economical to buy a string or package so you will have leftovers that will expand your collection. If you have problems locating a specific bead in local stores, check the Internet for inventories of the many online bead retailers.

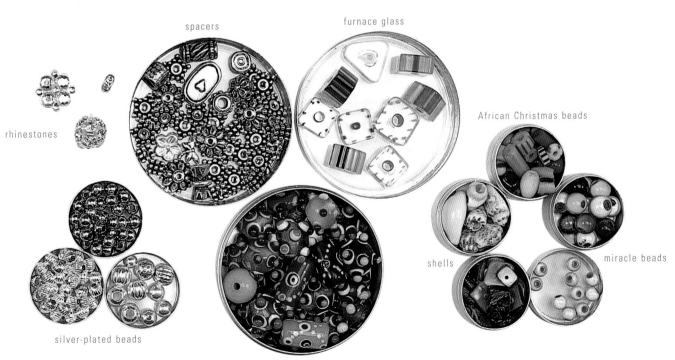

spacers

furnace glass

African Christmas beads

rhinestones

shells

miracle beads

silver-plated beads

art glass beads

natural beads

| **SEMIPRECIOUS BEADS** | Highly polished semi-precious beads are irregularly colored and patterned by the natural variations in the stone. Their increasing popularity means you can now find them in large craft supply stores. | **STONE CHIPS** | Like the semiprecious beads, stone-chip beads are made from a wide variety of stones such as jade, turquoise, and iolite. Their irregular shapes create an interesting juxtaposition to traditional round bead shapes. | **BONE AND HORN** | These rustic, irregular beads are carved from natural bone and horn pieces.

bead accents

| **SILVER BELLS** | Although these are not beads, silver bells are often used to accent beads. The small silver or brass bells come in a variety of sizes, and they're most commonly used with hemp to accent macramé jewelry. | **SEQUINS** | These inexpensive metallic-colored disks are often found with sewing notions and are available in a wide variety of shapes, sizes and colors. Their reflective surface makes the perfect frame for sewn seed beads. | **CHARMS** | Surprisingly inexpensive, charms come in a variety of shapes, sizes and finishes, including pewter, plated and sterling. Some charms are sold in themed sets, making it easy to group similar charms on a bracelet.

size chart

Round beads are easier to measure on a millimeter size chart and are usually packaged with the size printed on the package label or on the container in the bead store. You'll find many of the beads in this book aren't sized because they come from mixed-variety bags or don't have a uniform shape.

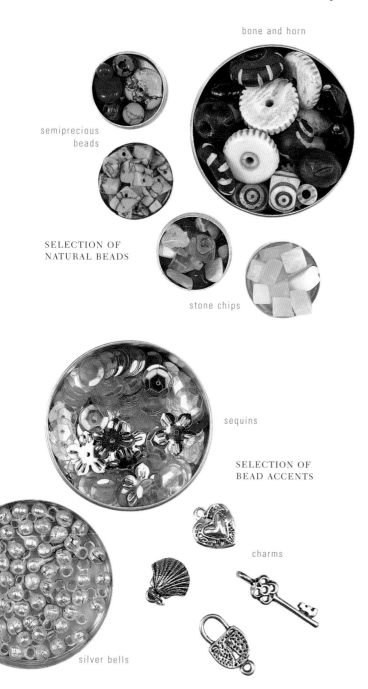

bone and horn

semiprecious beads

SELECTION OF NATURAL BEADS

stone chips

sequins

SELECTION OF BEAD ACCENTS

charms

silver bells

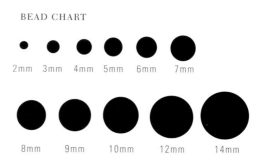

BEAD CHART

2mm 3mm 4mm 5mm 6mm 7mm

8mm 9mm 10mm 12mm 14mm

jewelry findings

Jewelry findings are an integral component of beading. Without the right crimps and clasps your beadwork will not be wearable. Take a moment to familiarize yourself with the options so that when you're shopping you'll select the right pieces for each project.

common findings

| CRIMP BEADS | Crimp beads are strung at either end of a strand to attach the clasp. Select the metal finish—gold or silver—that matches the beading wire and clasp. Crimp beads tend to blend in with a strand of beads.
| SMALL CRIMP TUBE | Small crimp tubes are used to attach small clasps or to position beads onto thinner beading wire. | STANDARD CRIMP TUBES | Standard crimp tubes are the most durable of the three crimping choices. The larger size allows the crimp to be folded over a second time to fully secure the beading wire ends.
| HEAD PINS AND EYE PINS | Head pins have a rounded flat end and eye pins have a loop end. Both serve to hold beads on the wire. The open wire ends of the eye pins are easily looped through ear wires to make earrings or through links to make beaded charms. They're sold in different lengths in both gold and silver metal finishes. The more expensive sterling varieties are the easiest to shape. | BELL CAPS | These are cup-shaped metal beads. A bell cap (not shown below) showcases a round bead by framing it on both sides. Select smaller bell caps for smaller beads and larger bell caps for larger beads. | SPACER BARS | Spacer bars eliminate twisting problems by allowing two or more strands to lay parallel to each other. Simply thread each strand through the bar at the same juncture in your beading. Select either understated bars that blend with the beadwork or ornate varieties that become focal points. Both varieties are commonly found with two, three or five holes.

Other findings include stemware hoops and pin backs (not shown below). STEMWARE HOOPS are wire hoops. Each has a loop on one end of the wire, and the other end is bent to fit through the loop after beads are slipped onto the ring. Select a hoop that matches the thickness of the glassware stem.

Plain metal PIN BACKS are inexpensive and are sold in different sizes. Stay away from the varieties that come with adhesive foam; jewelry glue provides better adhesion for jewelry making. It's a good idea to test the pin back for proper function before gluing it to your finished jewelry.

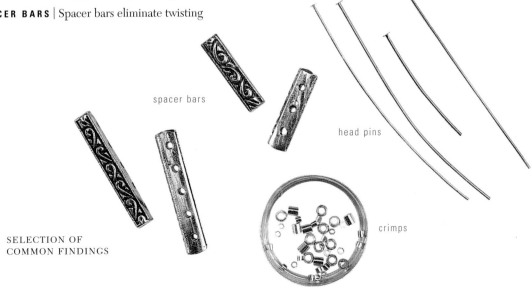

eye pin

spacer bars

head pins

crimps

SELECTION OF
COMMON FINDINGS

clasp varieties

A myriad of clasps is available; be sure to select one that matches the scale (size) and style of your beadwork. For instance, an ornate toggle clasp adds interest to a simply strung bead strand, whereas a small spring clasp better complements a delicate beadwork strand. As with all metal findings, pricing varies depending on whether the clasp has a metal finish or is pure sterling.

| **BARREL CLASP** | To close and open this clasp, one end is screwed into and unscrewed from the other end. The strand ends are either knotted or crimped to the wire rings on the outside of the barrel.

| **"S" CLASP** | The ends of the metal S hook onto the first and last links (or jump rings) to close the strand. Unhooking one end opens the strand. | **SPRING CLASP** | This is the most common and simple of the clasps. A small lever allows it to open and hook onto or unhook from a jump ring or the hole in an accompanying metal tab.

| **LOBSTER CLAW** | The lobster claw functions like the spring clasp, but the opening allows it to hook onto a larger jump ring or leather loop. | **"O" RING AND TOGGLE CLASP** | Each piece of the clasp is knotted or crimped onto a strand end. Fitting the toggle completely through the "O" ring then laying the toggle across the "O" ring fastens this clasp. | **HOOK AND EYE** | There are many ornate variations of the hook and eye clasp. Despite the differences in appearance, the clasping mechanism always functions the same: The hook end threads in and out through the eye opening to fasten and unfasten the strand.

| **MULTISTRAND CLASPS** | These clasps (not shown below) have added holes that make them the perfect choice for multistrand necklaces or bracelets. Simply thread and crimp each strand through one of the holes. These clasps help prevent twisting and knotting and give a piece a professional finish. | **JUMP RINGS** | Jump rings (not shown below) come in two varieties: open and closed. The open ring can hook onto links or jewelry findings. Be careful to open the ring laterally; if you spread it apart widthwise it will be hard to close it together again. The sealed ring is a secure choice to crimp to the end of a strand as part of the clasping system. Both are available in different sizes, in metal finishes and in sterling silver. | **SPLIT RINGS** | A split ring (not shown below) operates just like a regular key chain ring: One end is opened laterally, then the charm or chain link can be slipped onto the ring. Split rings are more costly than jump rings but provide a more secure connection. | **END CUPS** | End cups make a useful transition between the finished strand and the clasp. Perfect for thin beading thread, the end cup is strung onto the finished strand, and then the thread end is knotted. The knot will be securely hidden inside the cup, and the stronger metal crimp will hook onto the clasp. | **SPRING COILS** | Spring coils provide a transition from leather cord ends to the clasps. The cord ends are threaded into the open end of the coil, and then the first spring gets squeezed to secure the cord ends inside the coil. The clasp hooks onto the ring ends of the spring coils.

earring findings

Beaded earrings provide instant gratification as they're quickly assembled onto earring findings. I've used various kinds for pierced ears in this book, but it's a matter of personal taste. I used spring lever, French and kidney ear wires. The **SPRING LEVER** opens for placement on the ear and then springs closed for a secure fit (see pages 50 and 54). The **FRENCH EAR WIRE** is a simple fishhook shape that passes through the ear (see pages 32, 58 and 62). The **KIDNEY EAR WIRE** unhooks for placement on the ear and then rehooks for security (see page 52). Another type of earring finding (not used in this book) is the traditional **POST EARRINGS** with backings. The beads loop through a small ring that hangs below the stud.

spring coils

end cups

"O" ring and toggle clasps

hook and eye clasps

"S" clasp

spring clasps

barrel clasp

lobster claw

SELECTION OF CLASPS

threads & wires

The selection of stringing materials is crucial to the strength and appearance of finished beaded pieces. Follow the material guidelines for each project. You can always change the color, but stick with the specified product type to insure success.

beading threads

| TIGER TAIL | Tiger tail is one of the least expensive nylon-coated steel-core beading wires and is sold by the spool. Be sure not to purchase the thicker fox tail variety. Tiger tail doesn't knot and does have a memory, so try not to twist or kink the wire. | SOFT FLEX | Soft Flex has a stronger steel core than tiger tail and is also more flexible. It's sold by the spool in different thicknesses and weights. Although I've always crimped the ends, they can be knotted. | TRANSITE | This is inexpensive clear nylon fishing line that is sold by the spool. It's hard to knot, so use crimps for a more secure connection. | BLACK ELASTIC BEADING CORD | This heavyweight traditional beading cord has a white elastic core. This product is often found in the notion section of fabric stores. | STRETCH BEADING ELASTIC | Stretch beading elastic is strong and is sold by the spool in clear, pearl and black and in both .5mm and 1mm thicknesses. When color coordinated with the beads, it's almost invisible between beads. Use an overhand knot to join the ends. | BEADING THREAD | Beading thread comes in various colors and thicknesses. It's used with either traditional sewing needles or beading needles. If you have difficulty finding spools, purchase the necessary length by the yard at beading stores.

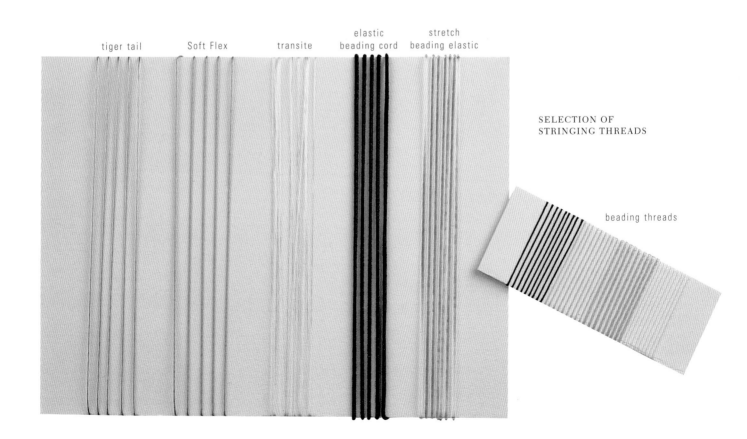

tiger tail   Soft Flex   transite   elastic beading cord   stretch beading elastic

SELECTION OF STRINGING THREADS

beading threads

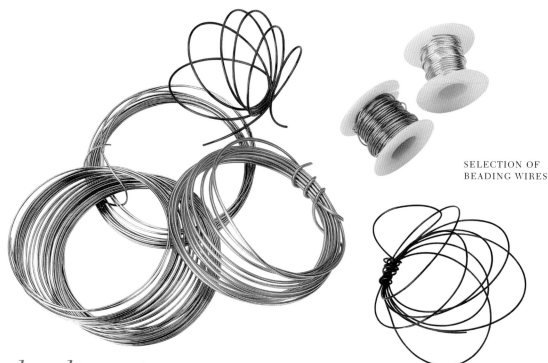

beading wires

All different sizes and colors of wire have been incorporated into the beading projects in this book. The advantages of beading with wire are that needles or knots aren't needed and beads can be quickly twisted or wrapped into position. The general rule when buying wire is the higher the gauge number, the thinner the wire, and, conversely, the lower the gauge, the thicker the wire.

|32-GAUGE BEADING WIRE| A very thin wire, the 32-gauge easily threads through small seed beads. It's usually available in both gold and silver finishes. Because it's so fine, twists and kinks can quickly cause the wire to break. To prevent this problem, follow the steps in "Preventing Twists in Wire," page 19. |STEEL WIRE| Inexpensive steel wire is available in varying gauges at craft stores and hardware stores. |COLORED WIRE| Color-coated wire comes in a variety of gauges and is available exclusively in craft and bead stores. To prevent the coating from chipping off, be cautious and use nonserrated pliers. More-expensive varieties of solid brass and copper wires are also widely available. Fun Wire, a brand of colored wire, is flexible and has a clear nylon coating that protects the color from chipping. |MEMORY WIRE| Memory wire is resilient coiled wire that is sold in bracelet, necklace and ring sizes. It's imperative to use either sturdy wire cutters or custom memory wire cutters on this wire.

other stringing materials

Other bead-stringing materials include link chain, leather, suede and hemp cord. LINK CHAIN (not shown below) is sold by the foot in bead shops and by the package in precut lengths with clasps in craft stores. Chains come in a variety of thicknesses. LEATHER AND SUEDE are sold by the yard in jewelry and fabric stores and by packaged lengths in craft stores. Select the cord by color and thickness, gauged in millimeters. HEMP CORD has an irregular rough and bumpy texture and is most commonly used for macramé knotted jewelry. It's made of natural tan fibers but it's also sold in a variety of dyed colors. It's an inexpensive cord with inherent natural variations. Be sure to look for the appropriate thickness gauged in millimeters.

suede

leather

round leather

hemp cord

tools

Of the many specialty tools on the market, only a few are really necessary to get started with beadwork. I strongly suggest purchasing round-nose pliers, needle-nose pliers, crimping pliers, wire cutters and a sharp pair of scissors. You should be able to make almost all the projects in this book using just these tools.

round-nose pliers

pliers and wire cutters

| ROUND-NOSE PLIERS | Round-nose pliers have two smooth, round, tapered ends that facilitate shaping wire into coils, circles or loops. | NEEDLE-NOSE PLIERS | Needle-nose pliers are commonly used in wire jewelry projects. They're perfect for holding the jewelry while wire ends get wrapped. Serrated pliers provide a tight grip but may mar the metal findings in the process. If you're working with precious metals or doing a lot of metal work, it's a good idea to use nonserrated pliers. | CRIMPING PLIERS | Crimping pliers have specialized grooved ends that work together to squeeze a crimping tube flat. If you're only flattening a crimp bead or a small crimp tube, you may be able to substitute a pair of needle-nose pliers. If you need to double crimp a standard crimp tube there's no substitute for a pair of crimping pliers (see page 20). It takes a little practice to get comfortable positioning the crimping tube in the appropriate grooves, but the resulting connection is very sturdy.

| WIRE CUTTERS | Save your scissors by using wire cutters to trim all your wires and link chains. It's safer to make a quick clip with wire cutters than to exert too much pressure with scissors blades. | MEMORY WIRE CUTTERS (OPTIONAL) | Memory wire is strong and its coils withstand stretching when it's repeatedly pulled on and off the wrist, neck or finger. Memory wire cutters easily snip through this heavy-duty wire.

scissors

Any good-quality scissors will work, but my scissors of choice are Fiskars Softouch Micro-Tip. They have small, sharp points that fit easily in tight places. The built-in spring is activated by a light touch on the handgrips. The center locking mechanism and plastic sleeve make them portable and easy to stow.

needles

I only use size 10 beading needles, as they're common and easy to find in craft stores. Before you begin beading, verify that the beading thread passes easily through the eye of the needle and that the threaded needle passes easily through the smallest of the selected beads.

I've specified regular sewing needles for a couple of the projects that don't use tiny seed beads. Just follow the above steps to make sure the needle, bead and thread work together.

crimping pliers

needle-nose pliers

wire cutters

small hammer

A small hammer is used to fold over the message rivets in the Candle Charms (page 118). A larger hammer would exert too much force and crush the thin metal.

eyelet setter

The eyelet setter spans between the rivet and the hammer. Its cone-shaped end encourages the sides of the rivet to fold out around the center opening.

glues

Ideally, beaded projects are stronger if they're strung, knotted or wired together. In the few cases in this book where glue is required, two different kinds are specified: G-S Hypo Cement and Aleene's Platinum Bond Glass & Bead Slick Surfaces Adhesive.

| **G-S HYPO CEMENT** | This glue has a built-in applicator. To keep the applicator tip clear, a tiny wire threads in and out of it when the cap is screwed on or off. It's perfect for accurately inserting a drop of glue into tight spots or over small knots.

| **ALEENE'S PLATINUM BOND GLASS & BEAD SLICK SURFACES ADHESIVE** | For larger areas, this adhesive is the perfect choice. It does require time to set, but when cured it creates a strong durable bond between glass beads and metal.

tape

Keep clear tape with your beading supplies. A small piece wrapped around the end of the stringing wire will help prevent accidents and keep partially strung strands secure.

Heavy-duty double-sided craft tape comes in different-sized rolls or whole sheets. It's a great shortcut that comes in handy when making beaded accessories and home accents.

storage containers

Plastic fishing tackle boxes are ideal for bead storage. Look for boxes with tight locking lids and sealed dividers that won't let beads slide out from under them. I use several boxes to organize my beads and sort them by variety (seed beads in one, glass beads sorted by color in another, stones and metal beads in a third). As your collection grows, continue to add boxes. Adjustable-divider tackle boxes are perfect for storing metal findings, threads, cords and wires.

work surface

Some people choose to purchase felted bead boards. I've found that stiff felt sheets sit better on my work surface and are easier to store. The texture helps prevent beads from rolling. Select a neutral gray or white sheet that doesn't hide the beads. If you use a variety of beads and want to keep them separated, purchase an inexpensive sectioned china dish from a bead store.

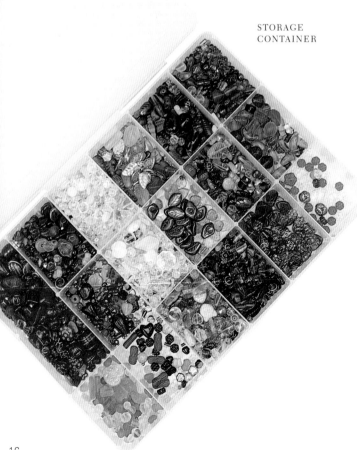

STORAGE CONTAINER

jewelry design

In the process of assembling this book, I stumbled across a few shortcuts and tips. They will help guide you as you select beads and customize the jewelry projects to suit your taste. I hope they will also help inspire you to create your own original jewelry designs.

1 | LAY OUT BEADS BEFORE STRINGING | Lay the beads out on a stiff felt surface in the desired pattern. Tape one end of the stringing wire and then thread the beads onto the open end. This allows you to see how the beads relate to each other when they're actually strung. If you need to make changes, you can slide the beads off either end without having clasps in the way. Be sure to slide the beads onto a felt surface so they won't roll away. Implement the same taping strategy for multiple strands to see how the strands work together before attaching the clasps.

2 | USE COLOR EFFECTIVELY | Color is a vital component of beadwork design. Even though there aren't any hard-and fast rules for good design, the following suggestions might help you.

If you choose to make a single-color jewelry piece, such as the Memory Wire Bracelets on page 72, add interest by selecting beads in range of that color from light to dark. Another choice is to complement the color with seed, spacer or "E" beads in neutral tones of silver or gold.

A surefire way to select colors is based on simple color theory. Complementary colors are opposite each other on the color wheel; the main pairs are yellow and purple, red and green, and blue and orange (see Charm Bracelets on page 38). Don't limit yourself to the exact color names. Be creative when you choose complements. For example, turquoise beads are greenish, and coral beads could substitute for red (see Double-Banded Watches on page 82).

3 | PAIR DIFFERENT BEAD VARIETIES AND SIZES | Another way to add interest to your jewelry design is to pair contrasting kinds of beads. For example, in the Liquid Silver Set (page 50), understated simple silver bugle beads are balanced with irregular natural stone beads.

4 | USE NONSYMMETRICAL DESIGNS | Sometimes breaking with traditional beaded patterns and symmetrical designs creates intriguing jewelry. The trick with nonsymmetrical design is to keep balance in the finished piece. In the case of the Leather & Rhinestone Bracelet (page 67), even though each bead grouping has different beads, each carries the same visual weight and is distributed along the length of the strand. Stones, charms and an ornate clasp heavily weight the front of the Pendant Clasp Necklaces (page 64). To offset this, the rest of the necklace is comprised of varying lengths of beaded stone, "E" bead or seed bead groupings.

5 | STRING RANDOM BEADS | The secret to random stringing is to not leave it to chance. Before you start, limit your design to several varieties of beads in only a few different colors. Even though you won't be working with a set beading sequence, attempt to evenly distribute the different varieties and colors between the beginning, middle and end of the strand.

JEWELRY SIZING

The finished length given with a project is only a suggestion (finished length includes the clasp). It's easy to customize the length to suit your tastes. Use the taping technique described in number 1 above to secure the beads on the strand before testing the fit around your neck, wrist or ankle. You can remove the tape and make any necessary adjustments by either adding or removing beads. This will ensure that your beadwork will fit perfectly before you attach the clasps.

techniques

Despite the tremendous variety in the appearance of the finished jewelry, accessory and home accent projects in this book, they share the same basic elements of construction. Because these techniques are frequently implemented, this section breaks them down and gives you detailed explanations. Take a little time to familiarize yourself with the knots, crimping processes and basic wire techniques before you get started. Once you're comfortable with even a few of them you'll find assembling the actual projects very simple.

tying a square knot

The square knot is the most common way to securely join two threads together. (It's the first step in tying your shoes and then repeated a second time)

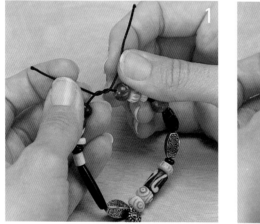
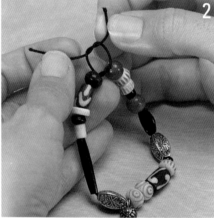

one • Take one end in each hand and then loop one end under the other and pull the ends to slide the knot where you want it.

two • Repeat step 1, looping one end under the other a second time, and then pull each end to tighten the knot. Trim the ends. For more security, add a drop of glue to the center of the finished knot.

tying an overhand knot

The overhand knot is most commonly used at the end of a sewing thread to stop the thread end from pulling through the fabric. In this book it's often used on either side of a bead (or grouping of beads) to position the bead on the strand.

one • Use a single strand of thread or cord. Wrap the strand into a looped circle. Thread one end of the strand through the loop and then pull tight.

NOTE: For the end of a sewing strand, thicken the knot by making additional overhand knots and positioning them over the first knot.

tying an overhand knot with a loop

This is a useful variation of the overhand knot. Instead of pulling the entire length of the
strand through the knot, pull out a folded end to form a tight loop. The loop often functions
as part of the clasp.

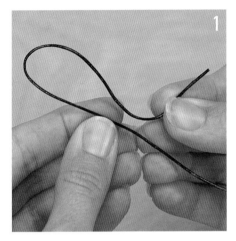

one · Fold the cord end down against itself. The
length depends on the size loop you want to make.

two · Wrap both cord thicknesses into a circle
loop under the fold.

three · Bring the fold around and through the
loop, then pull to tighten. If necessary, trim the cord
end where it comes out from under the finished knot.

preventing twists in wire

It's important to untwist any loops or twists in wires before pulling them tight and making them permanent kinks.
Kinks weaken the wire and can cause breakage.

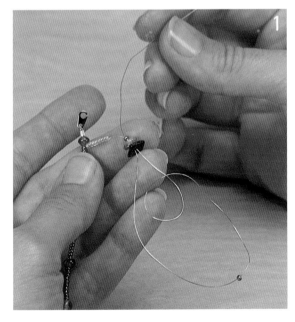

one · When pulling a length of wire through a bead, stop if
the wire loops.

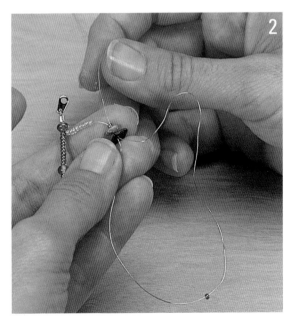

two · Untwist the wire and continue pulling the length
through the bead.

using crimp tubes

The utilitarian standard-sized crimp tube is commonly used to secure the strand ends to clasps. Its size accommodates most thickness of stringing wires and permits a double-folding technique that creates a strong connection.

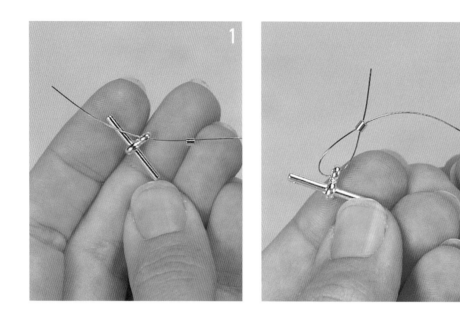

one · String one crimp tube followed by one part of the clasp onto the end of the strand. Position them about ½"–1" (1cm–3cm) from the end.

two · Fold the strand end back through the crimp tube. Pull the end to tighten the loop with the clasp.

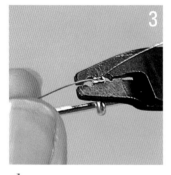
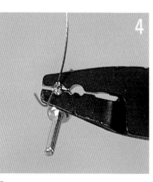
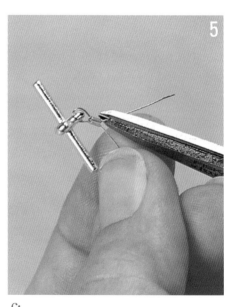

three · Separate the wires inside the crimp tube so that they rest against opposite sides of the tube. Clamp the crimping pliers over the outside of the tube, positioning the bumps in the tool with the center of the tube. Squeeze the crimping tool to flatten the tube's center and simultaneously trap the strings on the sides.

four · Use one of the rounded openings in the crimping tool to bring the string sides of the tube together, essentially folding the flattened tube in half.

five · Separate the strands where they emerge from the crimp tube, and then carefully cut off the remaining wire end.

Repeat steps 1–5 on the other end of the strand to attach the other half of the clasp.

using small crimp tubes

Small crimp tubes are so tiny that they're perfect for connecting small clasps onto light-weight, delicate jewelry. They also can be flattened onto either side of a bead for positioning.

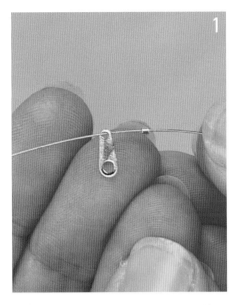

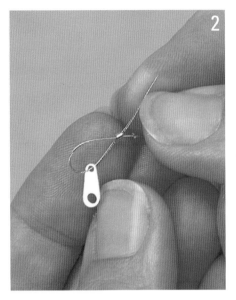

three · Clamp the crimping pliers onto either side of the crimp tube. Squeeze the pliers to trap the double thickness of wire in the flattened tube.

one · String one small crimp tube followed by one part of the clasp onto the stringing wire. Position them about ½"–1" (1cm–3cm) from the wire end.

two · Fold the wire end back through the crimp tube. Gently pull the end to tighten the loop that holds the clasp. Make sure the crimp is exactly where you want it, as this is the last opportunity to make positioning adjustments.

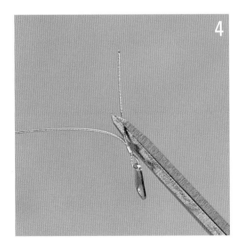

CRIMPING PLIERS AND ASSORTED CRIMPS

four · Separate the wires where they emerge from the crimp and then carefully cut off the remaining wire end.

Repeat steps 1–4 on the other end of the stringing wire to attach the other half of the clasp.

using crimp beads

The crimp bead is sized between a small crimp tube and a standard crimp tube. It's not as secure as the standard crimp tube because it can only be crimped a single time. Use crimp beads to attach clasps onto lighter-weight beading cord, transite and beading thread.

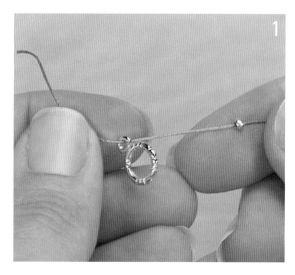 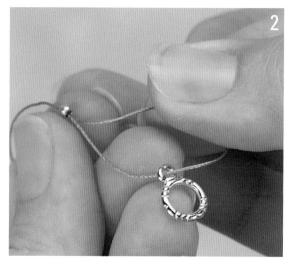

one · String one crimp bead followed by one part of the clasp onto the beading cord. Position them about ½"–1" (1cm–3cm) from the wire end.

two · Thread the end back through the crimp bead, and then pull the end to tighten the loop with the clasp. Make sure the crimp bead is positioned exactly where you want it.

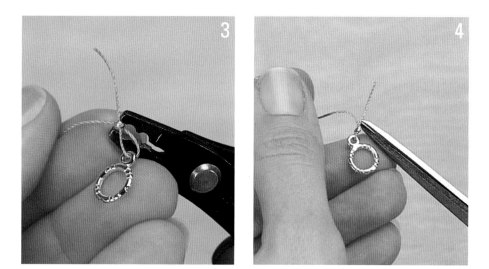

three · Clamp the crimping pliers onto either side of the crimp bead. Squeeze the pliers to trap the double thickness of beading cord in the flattened bead.

four · Separate the cords where they emerge from the bead, and then carefully cut off the remaining cord end.
  Repeat steps 1–4 on the other end of the cord to attach the other half of the clasp.

CRIMPING BEADS

Crimping beads often integrate into the jewelry's beadwork. In the Knotted-Thread Necklace on page 44, the gold seed beads look similar to the gold crimp beads, making a fluid transition from necklace to clasp. Similarly, in the Pendant Clasp Necklaces on page 64, the silver seed beads blend with the silver crimp beads so that it's difficult to discern where a connection has been made.

twisting wire

This easy technique is used to connect wires and position beads. It's a major component of
the Twisted-Wire Headband (see page 96) and the Wire-Wrapped Branches (see page 112).

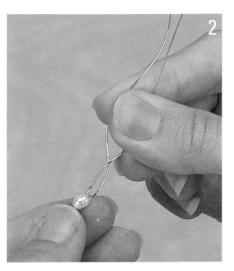

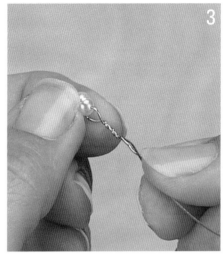

one · String one bead onto one end of the wire and position it according to the project instructions.

two · Hold the wire ends in one hand while you twist the bead with the other hand.

three · Make sure the wire is tightly twisted together directly under the bead.

looping wire ends

Shaping the wire end serves two important purposes. The first is to leave a safe rounded end
that prevents the beads from falling off. The second is to tighten the piece.

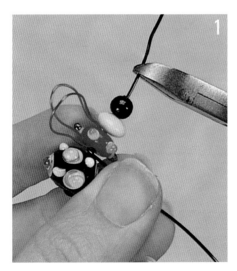

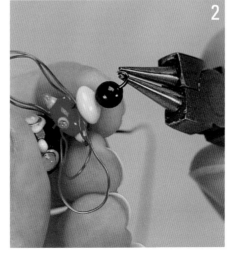

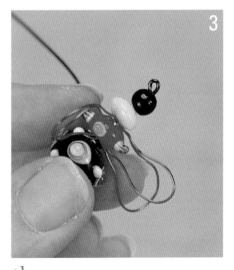

one · Slide the beads together to eliminate any slack, and then pull up on the wire end. Trim the wire ¼" (6mm) from the last bead.

two · Grab the wire end with round-nose pliers.

three · Loop the wire end back down against itself so it's positioned at the mouth of the last bead.

wrapping wire

Different varieties and gauges of wire are used in many projects, but the process of wrapping wire is almost always the same.

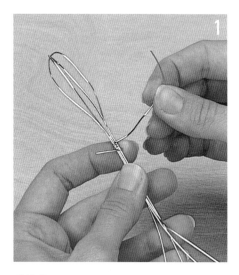

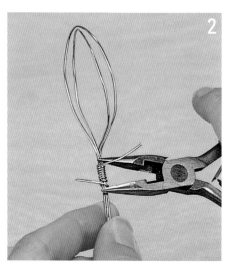

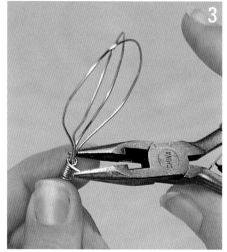

one · Hold one end of the wire against the surface of what you're wrapping, and then exert even pressure while tightly encircling the other end of the wire around the object. Position each wire wrap right against the last wrap.

two · Once you're finished wrapping, use needle-nose pliers to compress the wrapped wires and remove any gaps.

three · Use the needle-nose pliers to either push the wire ends into the item or flatten them against it.

spiralling wire

This is a handy technique to add to your repertoire. It turns any wire end into an ornate focal point. No matter how big or small the spiral is, the technique is always the same.

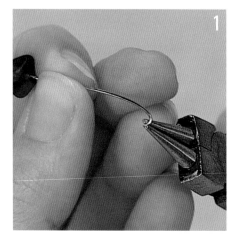

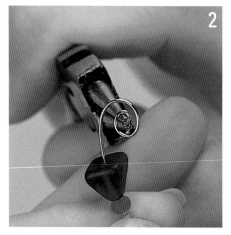

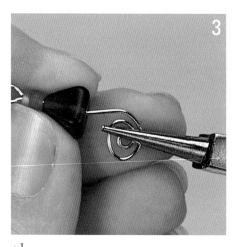

one · Grab the end of the wire with the tips of round-nose pliers.

two · Turn the wire end over into a tight loop. Rotate the pliers to enlarge the spiral and incorporate the length of the wire. The longer the wire, the larger the resulting spiral will be.

three · If necessary, flatten the spiral with round-nose pliers.

shaping head pins to create earrings

Follow these steps to create earrings to match any of the jewelry projects in this book. This technique is also used to transform beads into charms or pendants. The secure wire wrapping ensures a finished piece that can withstand daily wear. If necessary, eye pins can easily be substituted for head pins.

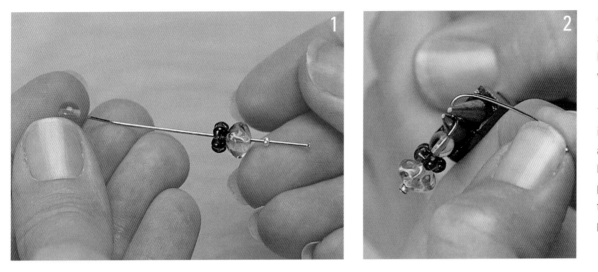

one · String a small sequence of beads onto the open wire end.

two · Begin shaping the wire directly above the last bead. Form a loop by wrapping the wire around the end of round-nose pliers.

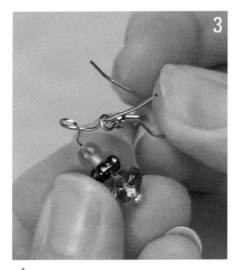

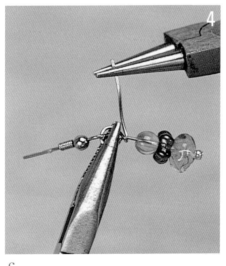

five · Trim the wire end flush against the head pin.

three · String the end of the earring finding onto the shaped wire.

four · Clamp the shaped wire with needle-nose pliers, and then grab the wire end with round-nose pliers. Wrap the wire end two to three times around the base of the newly formed loop.

jewelry

jam-packed with great projects and variations, this chapter features a vast array of styles and techniques to simply make your own beaded necklaces, bracelets and earrings. From casual to sophisticated and everything in between, it's easy to find a beading design to suit your own personal style.

Most of the projects use the basic techniques that are explained in detail at the beginning of this book. Once you've learned simple crimping and knotting, you're ready to start beading. Build on your success, and don't be intimidated by a project that might appear difficult. Each project is carefully broken into easy-to-follow steps.

Be inspired to look for new and unusual beads or to combine in different ways the ones you already have. Take advantage of your ability to customize the length, color and design of the pieces when creating your own jewelry. Your original creations are sure to garner compliments and requests from friends.

CHAPTER

modern glass bead chokers

MATERIALS

small crimp tubes

striped "E" beads

glass tube beads

spring clasp

16½" (42cm) tiger tail jewelry wire
(nylon coated, stainless steel)

crimping pliers

finished length: 15¼" (39cm)

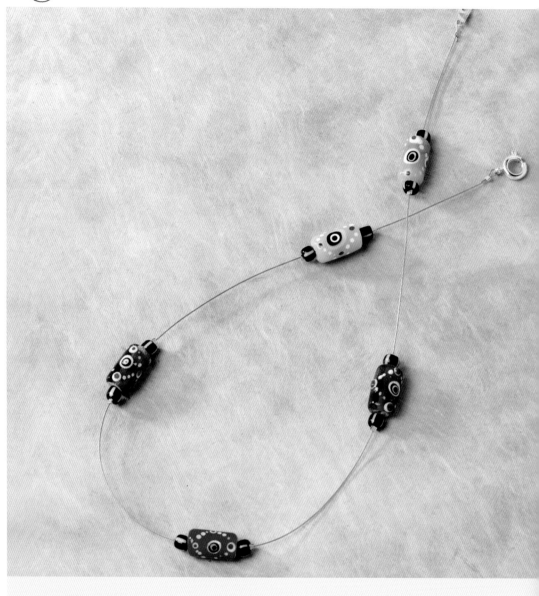

These beautiful crafted glass beads appear to be magically suspended on jewelry wire, but they're actually held firmly in place by small crimp tubes. The heaviness of the beads is contrasted by the lightness of the wire, creating a simple modern look.

ANOTHER SIMPLY
BEAUTIFUL
IDEA

Altering the space between each sequence of beads will change the appearance of your finished choker. The beads on the choker shown at left are spaced 1" (3cm) apart. If you select beads with small openings, you don't need to add "E" beads onto the choker. The "E" beads are used to keep the crimps from slipping inside large-opening beads. Finished length: 17¾" (45cm)

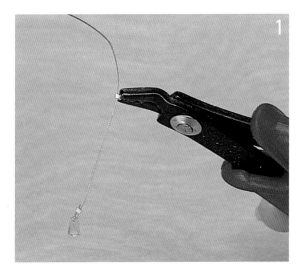

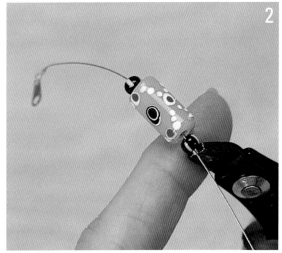

one · Use crimping pliers and a small crimp tube to attach one half of the clasp to one end of the tiger tail (see "Using Small Crimp Tubes," page 21). Position the first crimp 1½" (4cm) from the clasp and squeeze the crimp tube in place.

two · String the following sequence of beads onto the wire: one striped "E" bead, one glass tube, one striped "E" bead, and one crimp tube. Squeeze the crimp tube flat.

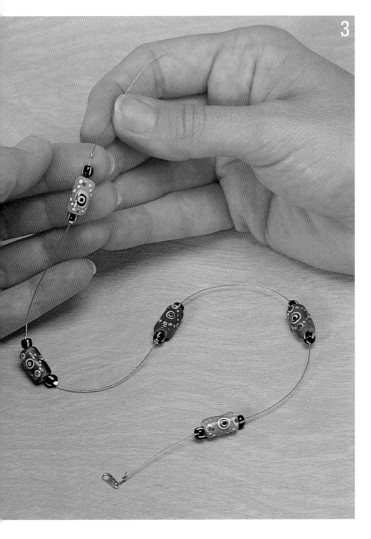

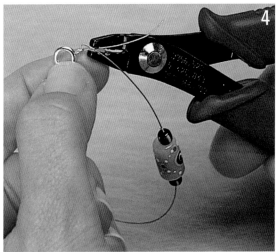

three · Space each additional sequence (crimp tube, striped "E" bead, glass tube, striped "E" bead, crimp tube) 2" (5cm) apart. Repeat the sequence four times.

four · Crimp the other half of the clasp 1½" (4cm) from the end of the last crimp. Trim any excess wire.

*tip > Be careful when storing your crimp choker. Tiger tail jewelry wire has memory and is hard to unkink if it gets knotted or twisted.

knotted-leather bracelet

MATERIALS

two 6mm round metal spacer beads

two round metal beads with large openings

large glass bead

antique silver toggle clasp

26-gauge wire

9½" (24cm) of size 2mm brown round leather

finished length: 8¼" (21cm)

The softness and sturdiness of the thick leather cord makes this jewelry perfect for everyday wear. Western accessories inspired the combination of leather, silver beads, wire and a decorative clasp. Select one-of-a-kind handcrafted glass beads to be the focus of the bracelet.

ANOTHER SIMPLY BEAUTIFUL IDEA

Follow the same basic steps to make the knotted-leather choker (shown at left), but you'll need to increase the length of the leather cord to 18" (46cm) and switch to a thinner "S" clasp that will lay flat behind your neck. Thread a silver heart bead and a small silver bead onto a head pin to make a pendant to string between the center glass beads. Finished length: 17" (43cm)

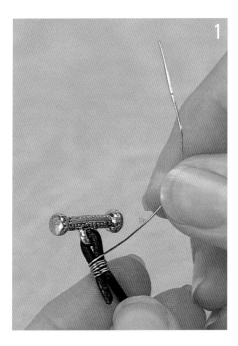

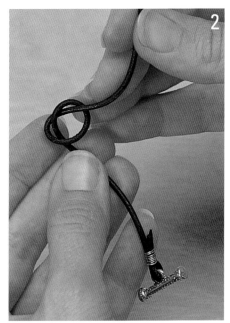

one · String the toggle side of the clasp onto one end of the leather. Fold ½" (1cm) of the leather end down. Use a 4" (10cm) length of wire to tightly wrap the double thickness of leather together.

two · Make an overhand knot (see "Tying an Overhand Knot," page 18) about 3" (8cm) from the clasp.

three · String one round metal bead, one metal spacer, one large glass bead, one metal spacer and one round metal bead. Slide a second overhand knot down the cord so that it rests against the last round metal bead.

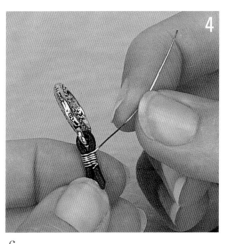

four · Pull ½" (1cm) of the leather end through the "O" ring clasp and fold the leather end down, leaving about 3" (8cm) of leather between the clasp and the last overhand knot. Wrap a second 4" (10cm) length of wire around the double thickness of leather.

tip > To prevent the wire from irritating the wearer's skin, be sure to fold and press the wire ends down in between the two thicknesses of leather.

pendant loop set

MATERIALS

BRACELET

seed beads

black 4mm crystal bicone beads

amethyst 4mm sim cat's eye beads

amethyst 6mm round crystal beads

olivine 6mm beads

3mm x 6mm metal dragonfly spacer beads

3mm x 6mm metal three-ring flower
spacer beads

pink 9mm glass bead

assorted small glass beads: purple, pink

green "E" beads

large natural stone bead

52" (132cm) white beading thread

size 10 beading needle

G-S Hypo Cement

finished length: 9¼" (24cm)

EARRINGS

two seed beads

six glass beads

two flower spacers

two 1½" (4cm) head pins

French ear wire

round-nose pliers

The polished stone focal point of this bracelet is also functional: It slides through a beaded loop to fasten the bracelet closed. A random mix of light- and heavyweight beads are strung onto a double thickness of beading thread so their weight falls naturally around the wrist.

ANOTHER SIMPLY
BEAUTIFUL
IDEA

The amber stone (shown on the bracelet at left) has a hole drilled through the top, so I tied it to a small loop of green seed beads and then completed the bracelet with a combination of black, green and amber-colored beads.

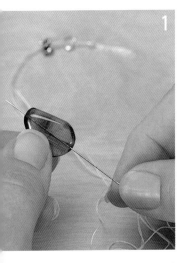

one · Thread the needle, and pull half of the thread's length through the needle. Tie the ends together with three overhand knots (see "Tying an Overhand Knot," page 18). String one seed bead, one pink glass bead, one three-ring flower bead and one large stone bead onto the thread.

NOTE: Always use a seed bead or other small bead on top of knots because a larger-holed bead will slip over the knot and off the strand.

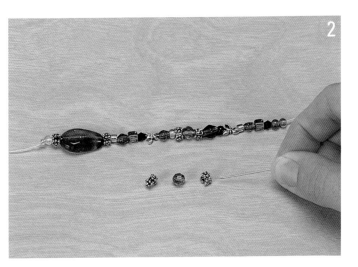

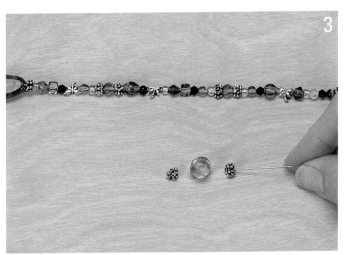

two · Next, string a three-ring flower bead, green "E" bead, purple glass bead, green glass bead, black bicone bead, and a dragonfly bead. Continue randomly stringing a mixture of black bicone, amethyst cat's eye, olivine, green "E", and small purple and pink glass beads, incorporating the following sequence three times on one side of the bracelet and twice on the other side: three-ring flower bead, amethyst 6mm crystal bead, three-ring flower bead.

three · Once you have 5½" (14cm) of beading, you've completed the first side of the bracelet. String a three-ring flower bead, pink 9mm glass bead and a three-ring flower bead.

four · Next, start with a black bicone bead and string 2¾" (7cm) of smaller glass, "E" and dragonfly beads. To shape the loop, thread the needle back down through the black bicone bead, then through the sequence from step 3 (three-ring flower bead, pink 9mm glass bead and three-ring flower bead).

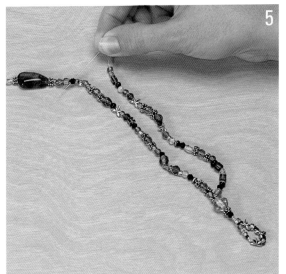

five · Bead the second side of the bracelet until it matches the length of the first side; remember to incorporate the two bead sequences from step 2. To connect the second side of the bracelet above the pendant, thread the needle down through the first black bicone bead. Tightly tie the string in an overhand knot below the bicone bead. Apply a dab of glue to each knot and trim the threads.

earrings

Cut ¼" (6mm) off the end of each head pin (see "Shaping Head Pins to Create Earrings," page 25). Slide a seed bead, three glass beads, and a flower bead onto each head pin. Thread the wire end of each head pin through the loop in one French ear wire, and then use round-nose pliers to bend the wire end over so it rests against itself.

33

daisy chains

MATERIALS

Czech glass beads: mahogany mini mix of seed, bugle and "E" beads

two crimp and ball end cups

barrel clasp

36" (91cm) black beading thread

size 10 beading needle

G-S Hypo Cement

round-nose pliers

finished length: 16³/₄" (43cm)

These delicate daisies are strung on lightweight beading thread so that they will fall naturally around the neck. Making the daisies is a two-step process: String half the petals and flower center in one loop and the other half of the petals in a second loop. Once you've learned the technique, there's no end to the beading variations. String multiple flowers one after another, or spread the flowers apart with long bugle beads. You can make the flowers larger or smaller by simply adding or omitting an "E" bead petal.

ANOTHER SIMPLY BEAUTIFUL IDEA

A single bead mix provided all the beads used in the Daisy Chains, including the accompanying variations (at left and on page 36). Bead mixes are usually packaged by color and include light to dark shades. Experiment with placing the lighter shade in the flower center and surround it with the darker shade petals. Or try the reverse to make dark-centered flowers.

daisy detail

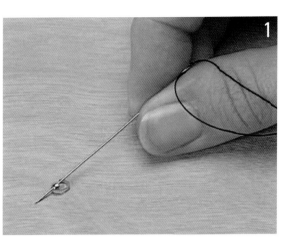

one · Thread the needle with black beading thread. Knot a seed bead onto the end of the thread using an overhand knot. Next thread the needle through the open ball side of the end cup. Slide the end cup down the thread until the knotted seed bead fits inside the ball. Squeeze a dab of glue into the end cup to secure the knotted thread.

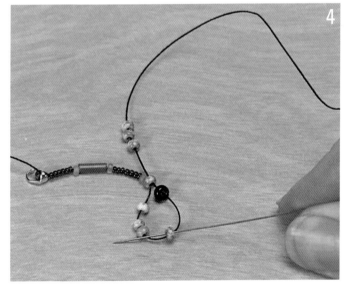

two · String six brown seed beads, one beige seed bead, one copper bugle bead, one beige seed bead, six brown seed beads and one beige seed bead.

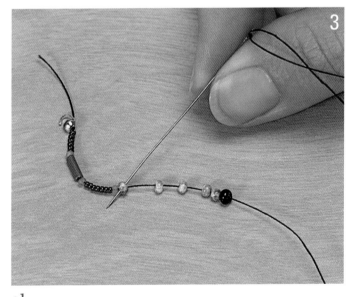

three · To make the flower, string five beige "E" beads (for the petals) and one brown "E" bead (for the flower center). Bring the needle back through the first beige "E" bead to form one half of the flower.

four · String three more beige "E" beads (for the petals). Bring the needle through the fifth beige "E" bead from step 3 and pull tight. Repeat the following sequence eleven times: one beige seed bead, the entire bead sequence (step 2) and the entire flower sequence (steps 3–4). To complete beading the necklace, string one beige seed bead, then repeat the beading sequence (step 2), omitting the last beige seed bead.

five · To finish the necklace, string the end cup (closed end first) and then a seed bead. Go back up through the seed bead to create a loop, and use the end of the needle to slide the seed bead down into the ball of the cup. Knot the thread and trim it. Place a dab of glue over the knot and around the bead to secure it to the end cup.

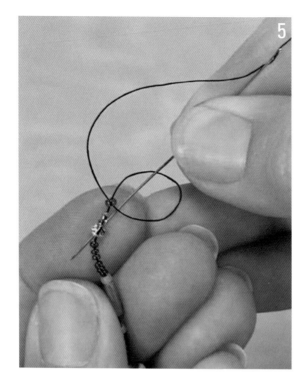

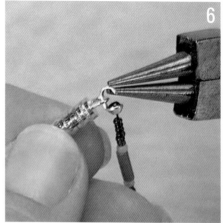

six · Thread the end cup crimp through the ring on one side of the barrel clasp. Use round-nose pliers to close the crimp and press the crimp end down inside the edge of the ball. Use the same technique to crimp the second end cup to the other side of the barrel clasp.

MORE SIMPLY
BEAUTIFUL
IDEAS

Bugle beads string together quickly, so if you're short on time string more bugles and make fewer flowers. The yellow lariat necklace (shown at right) is made with two separate strands that start with two flowers, then come together when they thread through the ebony "E" bead. The brown lariat (shown above) is made on a single strand. The beaded dangles are threaded onto the base of the center flower.

horn & bone bracelet

MATERIALS

goldtone metal finish beads: long tube, fancy deco, Arabic oval

8mm puffed heart beads

8mm and 12mm horn beads

assorted natural bone beads

assorted black glass beads

1" (3cm) gold head pin

10½" (27cm) beading cord elastic

tape

round-nose pliers

one · String a puffed heart bead (or substitute a small goldtone bead) onto a head pin. Grab the wire end with the round-nose pliers and shape the wire into a circle. Wrap the wire a second time around the pliers to complete a second circle, then slide the finished pendant off the pliers.

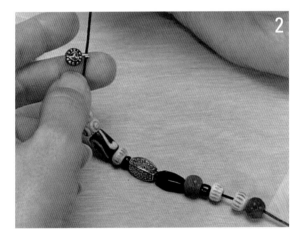

This chunky bracelet is strung together with a rustic mix of bone and horn beads. The large bead holes accommodate black elastic beading cord, making a sturdy finished bracelet that easily pulls on and off.

two · Place a strip of tape around one end of the elastic. String a random mixture of beads including the heart pendant onto the other end of the elastic, for a total beaded length of 6¼" (16cm).

three · Remove the tape, and tie the elastic ends into a square knot (see "Tying a Square Knot," page 18). Trim away the ends, and slide a bead over the knot.

charm bracelets

MATERIALS

five purple resin beads

five diamond-shaped glass beads

five glass heart beads

five gray oval glass beads

five purple round glass beads

fifteen 2" (5cm) head pins

five 6mm split rings

five assorted pewter charms

"S" clasp (with the jump rings removed)

6¾" (17cm) link chain

round-nose pliers

needle-nose pliers

finished length: 7½" (19cm)

L arge glass beads and silver charms jangle together on these playful bracelets. Pretty and practical, they're durable enough for everyday wear. The ends of the head pins are tightly wrapped, and the silver charms are securely looped in place with split rings.

ANOTHER SIMPLY BEAUTIFUL IDEA

Table and chair charms are paired with complementary yellow and violet glass beads to make this charming bracelet. Use the same bead and charm sequence; just substitute the different charm and bead varieties.
Finished length: 7½" (19cm)

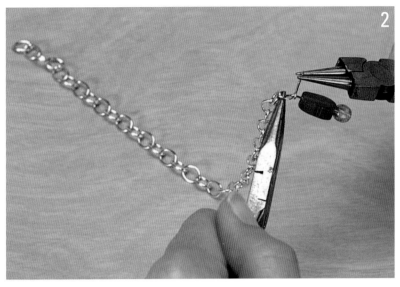

one · Slide a purple glass bead and purple resin bead onto a head pin. Shape the end of the head pin around round-nose pliers (see "Shaping Head Pins," page 25). Repeat four more times to create a total of five purple glass and resin bead shaped head pins. Make ten more shaped head pins, five with diamond-shaped glass beads and five with gray oval and glass heart beads.

two · Thread a purple glass and resin bead shaped head pin through the first link in the chain. Fold the wire down, and then twist the remaining wire back around itself before trimming.

three · Skip a link and then thread both a diamond glass bead shaped head pin, and a gray oval and heart-shaped head pin through the next link (third link). Thread a charm onto a split ring, and then thread the ring through the fifth link. If necessary, use round-nose pliers to clamp the ring back to its original shape.

four · Repeat steps 2 and 3, adding beads and charms to the remainder of the chain. Be sure to skip a link between each addition. Hook one end of the "S" clasp to the last bracelet link. To fasten the bracelet, hook the other end of the "S" clasp to the first link.

*tip > To have all the charms dangle the same way, place a charm on every other link. Interlocking chain links alternate directions, so by using every other link you're ensuring each charm will hang on one side of the chain.

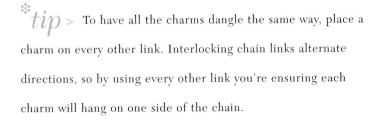

ladybug jewelry

MATERIALS

LADYBUG JEWELRY

two small crimp tubes

green seed beads

red and black 6mm glass bead

black "E" bead

off-white seed beads

black seed bead

flower bead

6mm spring clasp with 6mm ring

24" (61cm) bead-stringing wire, .012" (.31mm) diameter (for necklace)

needle-nose pliers

finished lengths:
(necklace) 15" (38cm);
(bracelet) 7" (18cm)

DRAGONFLY JEWELRY
(page 42)

pearl seed beads

purple rounded tube-shaped glass bead

two amber "E" beads

light purple seed beads

two round purple glass beads

flower bead

6mm spring clasp with 6mm ring

24" (61cm) bead-stringing wire, .012" (.31mm) diameter (for necklace)

BEE JEWELRY
(page 43)

black seed bead

tan seed beads

gold "E" bead

pearl seed beads

black and tan 6mm bead

flower bead

6mm spring clasp with 6mm ring

24" (61cm) bead-stringing wire, .012" (.31mm) diameter (for necklace)

These charming bug sets (see also the dragonfly and bee bracelets on pages 42 and 43) are inspired from nature. Light and colorful, they're perfect complements to summer fashions. The instructions for the necklace are shown on pages 41–42. Once you've made the necklace, creating the bracelet will be a breeze. For the bracelet, make three bugs separated by 1" (3cm) of seed beads, and omit the flower bead before the clasp.

ladybug detail

one · Use a small crimp tube to attach a spring clasp to the end of the stringing wire (see "Using Small Crimp Tubes," page 21). String green seed beads onto 7" (18cm) of the wire.

two · String the following sequence of beads onto the wire: a red and black glass bead for the body, a black "E" bead for the thorax and twelve off-white seed beads for the first wing. Thread the end of the wire back down through the first two off-white seed beads to shape the wing.

three · Thread the wire back up through the base of the black "E" bead.

four · String twelve off-white seed beads onto the wire for the second wing, then thread the wire back down through the first two off-white seed beads to shape the wing.

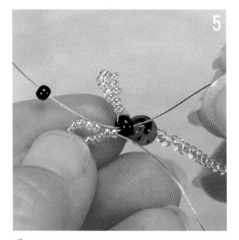

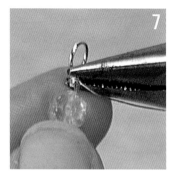

five · Thread the wire back up through the black "E" bead, then add a black seed bead for the head.

six · String green seed beads onto 6¾" (17cm) of the wire. Next, add one glass flower bead and one green seed bead.

seven · Use the second small crimp tube to attach a 6mm ring to the end of the wire.

finished length: 7" (18cm)

DRAGONFLY JEWELRY

dragonfly detail

• THE DRAGONFLY'S WINGS ARE MADE EXACTLY LIKE THE LADYBUG'S, although the dragonfly requires a second set. His elongated body is made with a rounded tube-shaped glass bead.

Start and finish the necklace using the same steps as for the ladybug, substituting pearl seed beads for the green beads. String the following sequence of beads onto the wire to create the dragonfly: a round purple bead, a rounded tube-shaped glass bead for the body, and an amber "E" bead. Next, shape the first set of wings using twelve light purple seed beads for each wing (see steps 2–4, page 41), then string an amber "E" bead and make a second set of wings. End with a round purple glass bead for the head. For the bracelet (shown above), see the basic instructions in the introduction on page 40.

bee detail

finished length: 7" (18cm)

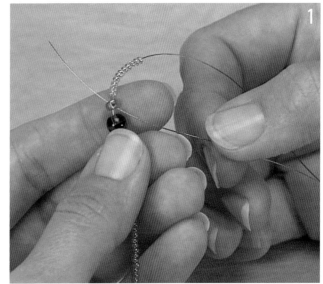

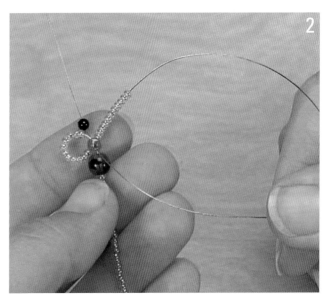

BEE JEWELRY

• THE BEE'S SMALLER ROUNDED WINGS are the simplest to make, and they perfectly complement its round little body. The steps at right show forming the bee's wings on the necklace (see steps 1, 6 and 7 on pages 41 and 42 to start and finish the necklace). For the bracelet (shown above), make three bugs separated by 1" (3cm) of seed beads. Omit the flower bead before the clasp.

one • Use a small crimp tube to attach a spring clasp to the end of the stringing wire. String tan seed beads onto 7" (18cm) of the wire. Next, string the following sequence of beads: one black and tan glass bead (for the body), one gold "E" bead (for the thorax) and eleven pearl seed beads (for the first wing). Thread the wire back through the base of the gold "E" bead to shape the wing.

two • For the second wing, string eleven pearl seed beads onto the wire, and then thread the wire end back up through the base of the gold "E" bead to shape the second wing. Add one black seed bead for the head. String tan seed beads onto 6¾" (17cm) of the wire followed by one glass flower bead and one tan seed bead. Use a small crimp tube to attach a jump ring to the end of the necklace.

knotted-thread necklace

MATERIALS

amber glass bicone beads

amber round glass beads

gold seed beads (use a large variety of
seed beads to fit over the sewing needle)

two gold crimping beads

"O" ring and toggle clasp

one gold donut bead

one large amber bicone bead

36" (91cm) heavyweight beading cord

sewing needle

crimping pliers

finished length: 20" (51cm)

D elicate and flattering, this knotted necklace requires few
beads and many knots to space them apart. The simplic-
ity of this technique is the perfect way to spotlight
impressed or guilded glass beads. Because the bare cord is
largely visible, color coordinating it with the beads is important.

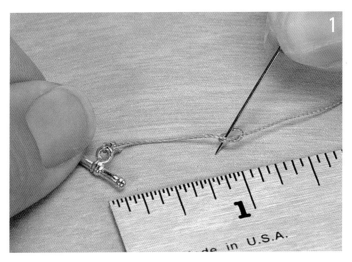

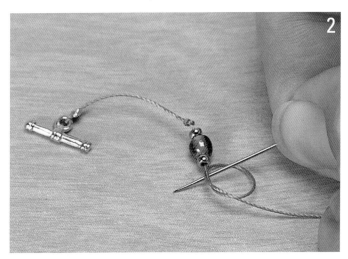

one · Use crimping pliers and a crimp bead to connect the toggle end of the clasp to one end of the beading cord (see "Using Crimp Beads," page 22). Tie an overhand knot in the other end of the cord (see "Tying an Overhand Knot," page 18). Position the tip of the needle in the center of the loose knot. Use the needle to guide the knot down the thread until it's 1" (3cm) from the clasp. Pull the positioned knot tight and remove the needle. This is the first knot of the bead/knot sequence. Use a ruler every time you tie the first knot to space each bead grouping 1" (3cm) apart.

two · String the first part of the bead/knot sequence: one gold seed bead, one amber round glass bead and one gold seed bead. Tie a second knot and use the needle to slide it against the last seed bead. To begin the second part of the bead/knot sequence, tie a third knot 1" (3cm) from the second knot. Then string an amber bicone bead. End with a fourth knot and slide it against the bicone bead. Repeat the bead/knot sequence (steps 1–2) two and a half more times to complete the first half of the necklace.

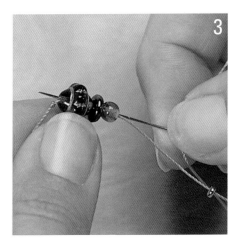

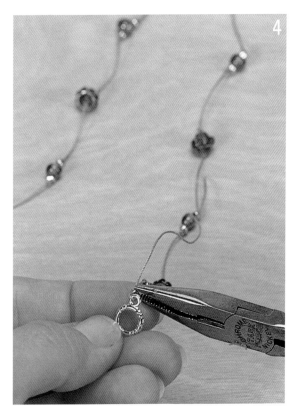

four · Beginning 1" (3cm) from the pendant, repeat the bead/knot sequence three and a half times to complete the second half of the neck-lace. Be sure to match the alternations between the amber round beads and the bicone beads so they correspond with the first side of the necklace. Use crimping pliers and a crimp bead to attach the "O" ring end of the clasp to the end of the necklace.

three · Tie an overhand knot 1" (3cm) from the last knot in the sequence. To make the pendant, string one large amber bicone bead, one donut bead, one amber round glass bead and one gold seed bead onto the cord. Thread the needle back through the amber round glass bead, the donut and the large bicone bead. Tie a second overhand knot and position it on top of the large bicone bead.

macramé bracelet

MATERIALS

BRACELET

five flat metal beads

round glass bead

20lb. blue hemp cord: one strand of 1 yard (1m), two strands of 2 yards (2m) each of hemp

craft glue

finished length: 7½" (19cm)

ANKLET
(page 48)

African Christmas beads (or substitute striped "E" beads and short glass tubes)

four "E" beads

5mm jewelry bells

glass bead (needs a large enough hole to accommodate four strands of hemp)

20lb. natural hemp cord: one strand of 2 yards (2m), one strand of 1 yard (1m)

I still find it hard to believe that my childhood experience of knotting macramé plant holders has proven useful twenty years later making hemp jewelry. This bracelet is perfect for beginners.

MORE SIMPLY BEAUTIFUL IDEAS

By simply changing colors and beads, each macramé choker takes on a different look. Make summertime jewelry with natural-colored hemp and drilled shell beads. The only limitation is finding beads that have openings wide enough to accommodate multiple strands of hemp cord.
Finished lengths: 13½" (34cm)

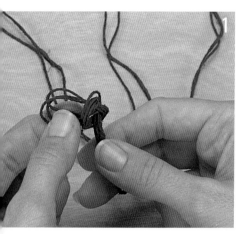

one • Fold each strand of cord in half and tie the centers of all three together in an overhand knot to make a loop (see "Tying an Overhand Knot With a Loop," page 19).

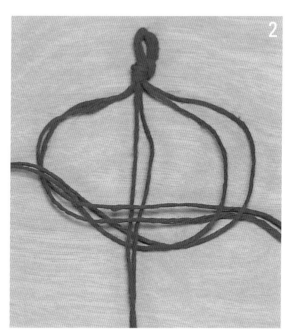

two • Organize the strands, positioning the two shorter lengths in the center with two long strands on either side. Follow parts a (shown at left) and b (step 3) to make a square knot.

PART A: Fold the two left strands over the center strands. Bring the two right strands over the left strands, thread them under the center strands and up through the loop in the left strands. Pull evenly on both ends to tighten the first half of the square knot and slide it up under the overhand knot.

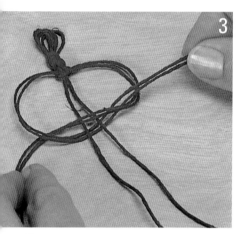

three • PART B: Fold the right strands over the center strands. Bring the left strands over the right strands, thread them under the center strands and up through the loop in the right strands. Pull evenly on the ends to tighten the second half of the knot and position it under the first half.

Repeat parts a and b seven more times to make a total of eight square knots.

four • Put glue on the ends of the two center strands of hemp to prevent fraying. Thread both center strands through a flat metal bead; slide the bead up under the last square knot. Follow the bead with another square knot.

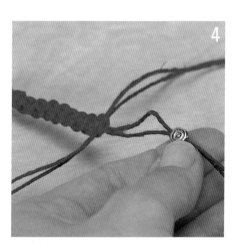

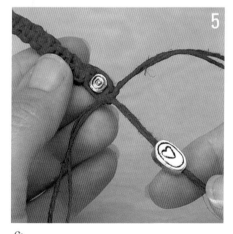

five • Thread another flat metal bead onto the two center strands and push it up under the last square knot. Repeat the process to string three more beads separated by single square knots.

six • Follow the last bead with eight more square knots. Tie all six strands into an overhand knot, then thread all the ends through a round glass bead. Tie all the strands in a second overhand knot to secure the bead and then trim the ends. To fasten the bracelet, thread the knotted-bead end through the starting loop made in step 1.

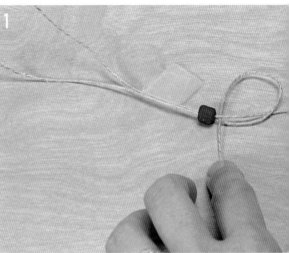

finished length: 10" (25cm)

MACRAMÉ ANKLET

• RINGS ON HER FINGERS AND BELLS ON

her toes she will make music wherever she

goes… The tinkling bells around this anklet

will bring smiles wherever you go. Lightweight

and colorful, it's the perfect casual summer

accessory for bare feet and sandals.

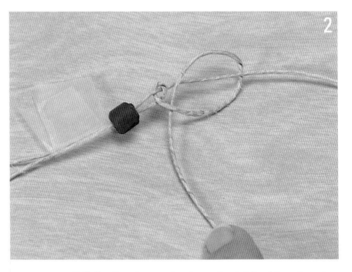

one • Tape the strand ends together 3½" (9cm) from the ends. Thread a glass bead through both strands, and slide it up under the tape. The shorter strand will always be threaded with beads and the longer strand will always make the knots and be threaded with bells. Begin the first half (PART A) of the knot with the long strand. Loop the long strand over and around the back of the short strand. Bring the end up to the left side of this first loop. Pull the end to tighten the first loop.

two • PART B: Continue making the second half of the knot with the long strand. Bring the end across the front of the first loop. Thread the end under, around and over the front of the short strand. Thread the end down between the two loops. Pull the end to tighten the second loop.

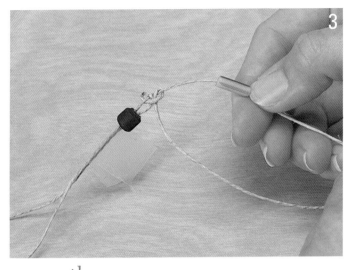

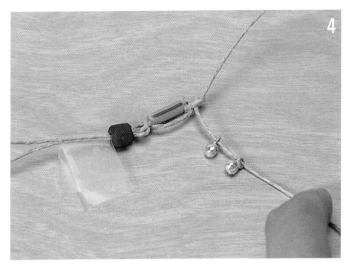

three • Thread an African Christmas (tube) bead onto the short strand of hemp.

four • With the long strand, tie another knot (parts a and b) around the short strand. Thread two bells onto the long strand.

five • Tie another knot with the long strand to secure the bells. Repeat the bead sequence fifteen more times: one African Christmas bead (short strand), knot (long strand), two bells (long strand), and knot (long strand).

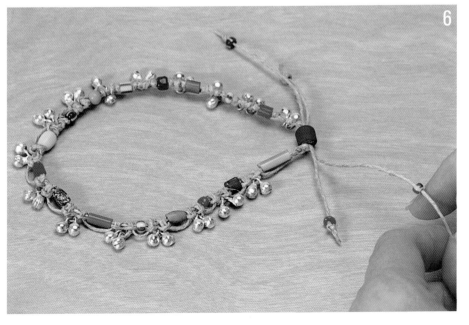

six • When you are finished with the bead sequence, thread the ends of both strands through the glass bead. Remove the tape from the first two ends. Thread an "E" bead onto each of the four strands. Secure each bead with a single overhand knot (see "Tying an Overhand Knot," page 18) and then trim the ends.

NOTE: The elongated strands slide through the glass bead to allow the anklet to enlarge when pulling it on and off. The "E" beads keep the ends from pulling through the glass bead while adjusting the fit.

liquid silver set

MATERIALS

BRACELET

silver bugle beads
(silver plate liquid traditional beads)

seed beads

semiprecious stone beads: quartz, carnelian,
fluorite, obsidian, jade, jasper, etc.

one carnelian daisy bead

crimp tubes

6mm spring clasp

2" (5cm) sterling head pin

9½" (24cm) Soft Flex, nylon-coated
stainless steel beading wire,
.014" (.36mm) diameter

crimping pliers

round-nose and needle-nose pliers

finished length: 8¾" (22cm)

EARRINGS

two rectangle beads of obsidian

two round beads of jasper

two 2" (5cm) sterling head pins

spring lever ear wire

A series of silver bugle beads strung together can give the illusion of a continuous silver strand. They create the perfect surrounding to bring out the inherent beauty of semiprecious stone beads. Each polished bead reveals the natural pattern and color variations of the stone. Enjoy selecting the beads one a time from a specialty bead store.

ANOTHER SIMPLY BEAUTIFUL IDEA

For this beautiful anklet, use 10½" (27cm) of beading wire and string a silver seed bead before and after each silver bugle bead. Add a carnelian daisy bead to the end of the clasp. Finished length: 9½" (24cm)

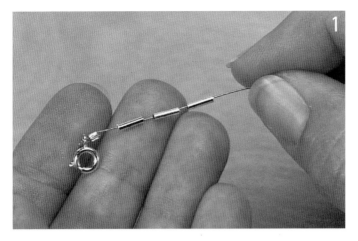

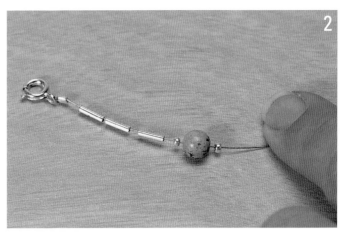

one · Use crimping pliers and a crimp tube to attach the spring clasp to one end of the beading wire (see "Using Crimp Tubes," page 20). Begin the beading sequence by stringing three silver bugle beads onto the wire.

two · Continue the beading sequence by stringing one seed bead, one semi-precious stone and one seed bead.

three · Repeat the bead sequence (three silver bugle beads, one seed bead, one semiprecious stone and one seed bead) six times, then string three silver bugle beads. Use crimping pliers and a crimp tube to attach the other part of the clasp to the wire.

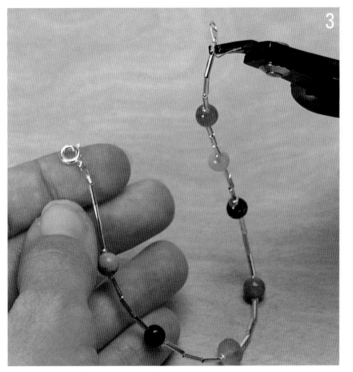

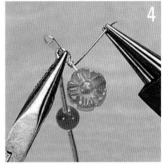

four · Slide a carnelian daisy onto the head pin (see "Shaping Head Pins," page 25). Bend the end of the head pin over, then loop the wire end through the end of the clasp. Complete the wire loop, then wrap the wire back around itself two times before trimming the excess wire.

*tip > If you are using two of the same type of semiprecious stone bead, space them apart so that they are distributed between the other varieties of semi-precious stone beads.

earrings

Slide one obsidian rectangle bead followed by one jasper bead onto a head pin (see "Shaping Head Pins to Create Earrings," page 25). Bend the end of the head pin over and then thread it through a spring lever ear wire. Complete the wire loop, then wrap the wire back around itself two to three times before trimming the excess wire. Repeat for the second earring.

beaded daisy set

MATERIALS

NECKLACE

silver "E" beads

seed beads: opaque turquoise, teal luster

6mm ring

spring clasp

2mm spring coils

24" (61cm) of 32-gauge beading wire

16½" (42cm) suede lace

needle-nose pliers

finished length:17" (43cm)

EARRINGS

silver seed beads

seed beads: opaque turquoise, teal luster

¾" (2cm) kidney ear wire

15" (38cm) of 32-gauge beading wire
(for each earring)

ANOTHER SIMPLY
BEAUTIFUL
IDEA

Create your own playful pendant with seed beads. The flower may appear complex, but it's simply five two-colored beaded loops wired around a silver bead flower center. The comfortable suede lace choker complements the intricate beaded daisy. This is one of the few projects where the earrings are made almost exactly like the pendant. The size of the center beads and the quantity of petal beads just get changed.

Experiment making flowers in other colors. Be sure to select two different shades of seed and "E" beads to make the flower more interesting. If you prefer gold to silver, switch to gold beads and findings. Finished length: 17" (43cm)

one · String five silver "E" beads onto one end of the beading wire and then twist the ends together to make a round flower center. Cut off the short end.

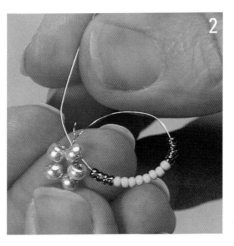

two · String the first petal sequence onto the wire: four teal seed beads, eight turquoise seed beads and four teal seed beads. Thread the wire back through the first silver "E" bead.

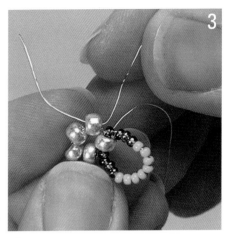

three · Thread the wire through the fifth silver bead and then string the petal sequence onto the wire. Thread the wire end back through the fifth silver bead to shape the second petal. Repeat this step, threading the wire into the fourth silver "E" bead to make a third petal.

four · Continue working in this fashion, beading petals for the third and second silver "E" beads. Before threading the wire end back into the second silver "E" bead, string a 6mm ring onto the beaded wire. To finish, wrap the wire end three times around the flower center wire, and then trim the wire.

five · String the beaded daisy onto the suede lace. Thread a spring coil onto each end of the lace. Use needle-nose pliers to squeeze the last wire coil of each spring coil, trapping the suede ends inside the springs. Hook a spring clasp onto the ring end of one of the spring coils.

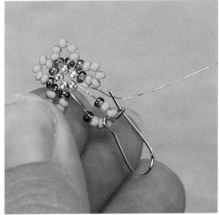

earrings Follow the basic instructions for making the daisy. Use silver seed beads for the flower center, and substitute the following sequence to make the petals: one teal seed bead, four turquoise seed beads and one teal seed bead. Thread a kidney wire onto the last beaded petal before threading the wire end through the last silver seed bead. Wrap the wire two times around the flower center wire before trimming.

semiprecious stone set

MATERIALS

BRACELET

semiprecious stone chips
(jade and assorted purple stone chips)

crimp tubes

charm

spring clasp

8" (20cm) Soft Flex, nylon-coated
stainless steel beading wire,
.014" (.36mm) diameter

crimping pliers

finished length (bracelet):
7½" (19cm)

EARRINGS

silver seed beads

peridot beads

jade and purple stone chips

2" (5cm) sterling silver head pin

spring lever ear wire

round- and needle-nose pliers

Natural stones create the perfect setting for a thought-provoking charm. The subtle color palette complements the simple silver chain. Select sterling silver jewelry findings to match and Soft Flex wire to support the investment in semiprecious beads. For the earrings, use spring lever ear wire. Spring lever earrings have a secure fit, making them a good choice when using more-expensive semiprecious stone beads.

ANOTHER SIMPLY BEAUTIFUL IDEA

Stretch the natural stones by stringing a single seed bead between each peridot bead for this bracelet (shown at left). If you prefer, position the charm by the clasp instead of in the center of the strand.
Finished length: 7½" (19cm)

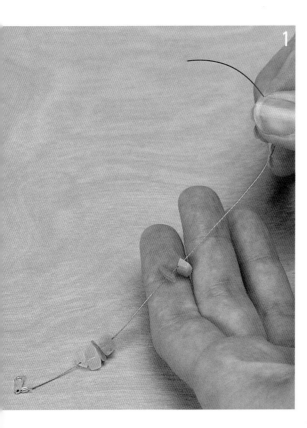

one · Use crimping pliers and a crimp tube to attach one end of the wire to one part of the clasp (see "Using Crimp Tubes," page 20). String a random mix of jade and purple semi-precious stone chips onto the wire.

two · When you have a beaded length of 3½" (9cm), string the charm onto the wire.

three · String stone chips onto another 3½" (9cm) of the wire to complete the length of the bracelet. Use crimping pliers and a crimp tube to attach the end of the wire to the other part of the clasp.

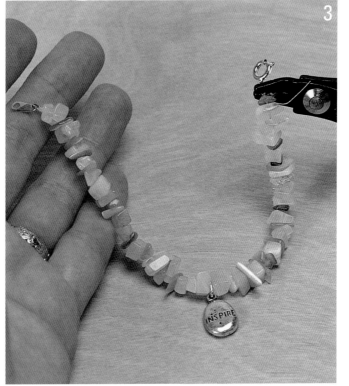

earrings

String the following sequence onto a head pin: one silver seed bead, one peridot bead and two stone chips. Shape the end of the pin, thread it through the earring, and wrap the wire back around itself twice before trimming the end (see "Shaping Head Pins to Create Earrings," page 25). Repeat the process to make a second earring.

multistrand stretch bracelets

MATERIALS

glass-inside rainbow bugle beads

five-hole scroll silver spacers

five 12" (30cm) strands of size .5mm clear stretch beading elastic (such as transparent Stretchy Illusion cord)

G-S Hypo Cement

clear tape

It would be easy to forget that you're wearing a multistrand stretch bracelet if it didn't catch the light with every turn of your wrist; it's so lightweight and comfortable. The scroll spacer bars keep the strands in order and add an element of drama by framing the beads.

If you're short on time, longer bugle beads string together quickly so substitute them for the rainbow bugles. For a more ornate design, string contrasting pearl beads and seed beads between a pair of silver spacers at the center of the piece (as seen on the bracelet at left). If you choose to make the choker (shown at top left), you'll need to attach a clasp to either end to finish the piece.

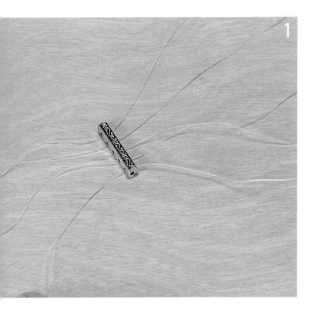

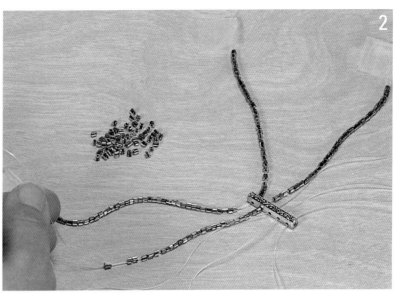

one · Thread a strand of clear stretch beading elastic into each hole in the five-hole spacer. Center the spacer in the middle of the elastic lengths.

two · Start with the top strand. String seed beads onto about 3" (8cm) of the elastic on each side of the spacer. Tape the end of each completed bead strand so the beads won't fall off. Repeat this process for the four remaining strands.

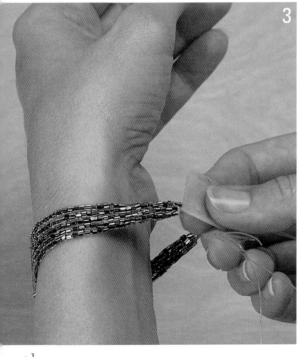

three · Holding the taped ends together, wrap the bracelet around your wrist to gauge the fit. If necessary, adjust the amount of beads so that the bracelet will fit snugly around your wrist.

four · When you're satisfied with the fit, remove the tape from the ends and lay the bracelet face down on your work surface. Starting with the first strand, thread one end through each side in the top of the second spacer. Bring the ends together in the middle of the spacer and tie a square knot (see "Tying a Square Knot," page 18). Repeat this process for the four remaining strands. When all of the strands are knotted, trim the elastic ends and apply a dab of glue to secure each knot.

illusion set

MATERIALS

NECKLACE

a combination of the following glass seed, "E" and bugle beads (or substitute a prepackaged white mix): iridescent, opaque, glitter and pearl

four crimp beads

silver barrel clasp

six 36" (91cm) strands of transite (nylon fishing line)

needle-nose pliers

finished length: 18" (46cm)

EARRINGS

two crimp beads

white glass bead mix (see above)

eight small crimp tubes

Sterling silver French ear wire

four 5" (13cm) lengths of transite (nylon fishing line)

ANOTHER SIMPLY BEAUTIFUL IDEA

Cascades of beads are strung onto multiple strands of transite, making a lightweight, comfortable necklace. Double stringing the beads suspends them between two strands. It's not an illusion that this randomly strung necklace is simple to bead, and you can use leftover beads and transite to create matching earrings.

Once you're comfortable with the technique, you may decide you prefer a wider necklace with an third set of transite lengths, or for a more understated look, use only one set of transite lengths instead of two. Finished length: 18" (46cm)

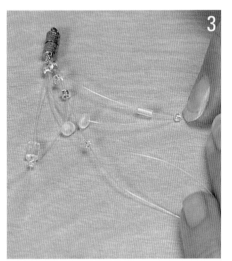

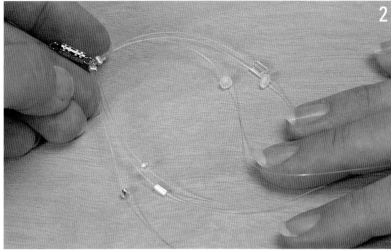

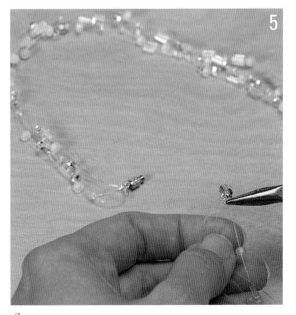

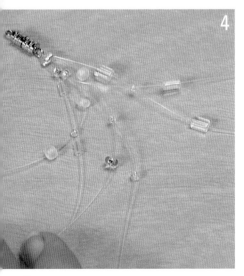

one · Group the ends of three transite strands together and then thread them through a crimp bead and one side of a barrel clasp and then back down through the crimp bead. Use the needle-nose pliers to squeeze the crimp bead flat (see "Using Crimp Beads," page 22). Trim the ends of the transite. Repeat the process with the three remaining lengths of transite, crimping them to the same part of the barrel clasp with the first grouping.

two · String a bead onto each of the six strands.

three · Randomly pair the strands together to make three groupings. Double string one bead onto each pair of strands.

earrings

Thread two 5" (13cm) strands of transite through the ear wire. Pull the strands partway through the ear wire so that half the length is on one side and the other half is on the other side. Thread all four transite ends through a crimp bead, and then slide the crimp bead up under the ear wire. Use the pliers to squeeze the crimp bead flat. String beads and one small crimp tube onto each of the four transite ends. Use the pliers to squeeze each crimp tube flat and then trim the excess transite. Repeat the process to make a second earring.

four · Ungroup the strands, and string a bead onto each of the six strands. Repeat step 3, then alternate between the single- and double-strand beading until you have 17" (43cm) of beaded length.

five · Group the strands into two groups of three strands in each. Use needle-nose pliers and a crimp bead to attach each group to the other side of the barrel clasp (see step 1).

mother's bracelets

MATERIALS

four 3.5mm silver beads

two 4.5mm silver beads

6mm silver bead

silver letter beads

two 8mm crystal birthstone beads
(for each child)

eight clear crystal discs

eight rhinestone discs

toggle clasp

9" (23cm) Soft Flex, nylon-coated stainless
steel beading wire, .014" (.36mm) diameter

finished length: 8" (20cm)

MORE SIMPLY
BEAUTIFUL
IDEAS

Keep your children near even when you're at work. These personalized bracelets combine your child's birthstone with rhinestones and silver beads. Make a thicker bracelet by making a strand for each child's name or place the names together on a single strand for a thinner bracelet.

Layered glass furnace beads and sparkling crystal beads are paired to make these beautiful bracelets. Because the combination of beads is visually interesting, I chose a limited color palette and paired them with a simple clasp, pearls, rhinestone discs, and plain silver beads.
Finished lengths: 7½" (19cm)

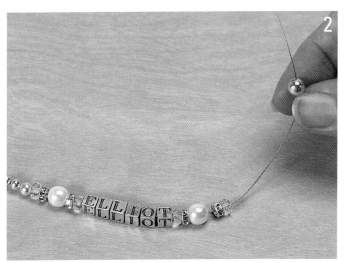

one · Use a crimp tube to attach the "O" ring to one end of the wire (see "Using Crimp Tubes," page 20). String this beginning sequence onto the wire: two 3.5mm beads, one 4.5mm bead, one crystal disc, one rhinestone disc, one birthstone and one rhinestone disc.

two · Add a crystal disc, spell out the child's name in alphabet beads, and follow with another crystal disc. Sandwich one birthstone between two rhinestone discs. To separate children's names, string a crystal disc, 6mm silver bead and a crystal disc.

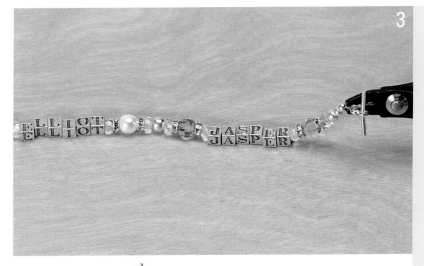

three · String a rhinestone disc, one birthstone, one rhinestone disc, a crystal disc, letters that spell the next name, and one crystal disc. To finish the bracelet, string the beginning sequence from step 1 in reverse (rhinestone disc, birthstone, rhinestone disc, crystal disc, 4.5mm bead, two 3.5mm beads). Attach the toggle end of the clasp using a crimp tube.

CRYSTAL BIRTHSTONE CHART

MONTH	CRYSTAL
January	Garnet (dark red)
February	Amethyst (dark purple)
March	Aquamarine (light blue)
April	Crystal (clear)
May	Emerald (dark green)
June	Light Amethyst (light purple)
July	Ruby (dark red)
August	Peridot (light green)
September	Sapphire (medium blue)
October	Rose (pink)
November	Topaz (brown/orange)
December	Blue Zircon (turquoise)

Semiprecious birthstones can be expensive, so consider using crystal beads. The chart above gives the suggested crystal and color that corresponds with each month.
(source: www.bestbuybeads.com/colorchart.asp)

four-strand necklace set

MATERIALS

NECKLACE

seed beads: tan, blue, red, green

"E" beads: tan, blue, red, green

cube beads

eight small crimp tubes

antique silver hook and eye four-hole clasp

four 19" (48cm) strands of bead-stringing wire, nylon-coated stainless steel, .012" (.31mm) diameter

crimping pliers

clear tape

finished length (necklace): 16¼" (41cm)

EARRINGS

two tan seed beads

two red "E" beads

two blue pyramid-shaped glass beads

2" (5cm) eye pin

French ear wire

round-nose pliers

I've been drawn to these seed and "E" beads for awhile. Their sand-washed appearance reminds me of sea glass. They're packaged and sold by color, but each bead has individual tonal variations. The simple design of this necklace showcases the subtleties of the beads. The only ornamentation is the rustic clasp that brings the four colorful strands together. These fun little dangling earrings are the perfect complement to the four-strand necklace. The triangle bead shares the same finish and color as the blue seed and "E" beads in the necklace.

ANOTHER SIMPLY BEAUTIFUL IDEA

These matching earrings incorporate the very same beads that are used in the necklace. String the following sequence onto each eye pin: three red seed beads, a blue "E" bead, and a green cube bead. Use round-nose pliers to spiral the wire ends.

one · Use a small crimp tube to attach one end of each strand of wire to a hole in the eye portion of the four-hole clasp (see "Using Small Crimp Tubes," page 21).

two · String a short length of random-colored seed beads onto each wire. String one of the following four sequences onto each wire: a single "E" bead, two same-colored "E" beads with a third different-colored "E" bead in-between, two same-colored cube beads with a different-colored "E" bead in between, or two same-colored "E" beads with a different-colored cube bead in-between. Return to stringing random seed beads, stopping to incorporate one of the above sequences approximately 10–12 times per string. Bead a total of 15¼" (38.7cm) of the first strand, 15½" (39cm) of the second, 15¾" (40cm) of the third and 16" (41cm) of the fourth. Place a strip of tape on the end of each finished strand so that the beads won't fall off while you work on the remaining strands.

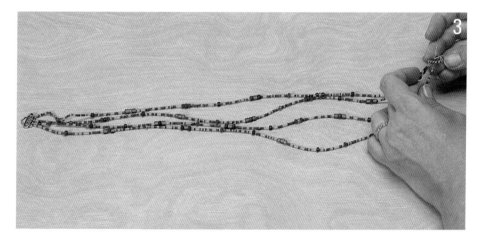

three · Remove the tape and use a small crimp tube to attach the wire end of the first strand to the top hole in the hook portion of the four-hole clasp. Repeat the process to connect the remaining three wires to the corresponding holes in the clasp.

earrings

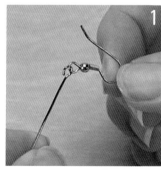

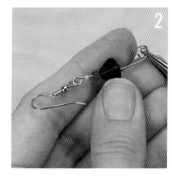

two · Slide one tan seed bead, one red "E" bead and one blue pyramid bead onto the end of the eye pin. Use the round-nose pliers to spiral the wire end of the eye pin (see "Spiralling Wire," page 24). Repeat the process to assemble a second earring.

one · Hook the wire end that forms the circle of the eye pin through the hole in the French ear wire. Use the round-nose pliers to close the opening in the eye pin.

pendant clasp necklaces

MATERIALS

**PENDANT CLASP
NECKLACE**

silver "E" beads

silver seed beads

assorted rocks: jasper, turquoise,
amethyst, fluorite

polished stone bead

metal spacer bead

crimp beads

square prayer box charm

silver wire and ball "S" hook

two 2" (5cm) eye pins

5½" (14cm) suede lace

48" (122cm) beading thread

round- and needle-nose pliers

crimping pliers

size 10 beading needle

finished length: 18" (46cm)

**LOCK AND KEY
PENDANT CLASP**
(page 68)

silver "E" beads

silver seed beads

assorted rocks: peridot, jasper, turquoise

polished stone bead

metal spacer bead

crimp beads

lock and key toggle charms

heart charm

three 2" (5cm) head pin

silver wire and ball "S" hook

5½" (14cm) brown suede lace

48" (122cm) beading thread

These intriguing necklaces (see page 66 for variation) are created with a fascinating mix of natural stones, beads, charms and an ornate clasp. At first glance the combination of elements gives the impression that the necklaces are complicated to string. Don't be misled: The steps are easy to follow.

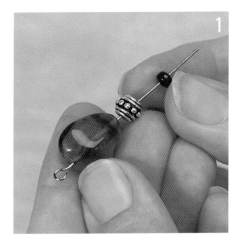

one · To create the pendant, string the following sequence onto an eye pin: one polished stone bead, one metal spacer and one small jasper bead.

two · Shape the wire end of the eye pin around the round-nose pliers and then thread the wire end through the small hole in the eye part of the clasp. Wrap the wire back around itself before trimming the end (see "Shaping Head Pins," page 25).

three · Thread the suede lace through the eye section of the pin and through the prayer box, then tie the lace ends in a square knot (see "Tying a Square Knot," page 18). Set aside the pendant.

four · Loop the eye section of a second eye pin through the hook part of clasp. If necessary, use round-nose pliers to bend the eye pin back into its rounded shape.

five · String the following onto the eye pin: one turquoise bead, two jasper beads and two silver "E" beads. Shape the wire eye pin end around the round-nose pliers to create a loop. Secure the wire end by wrapping it twice below the loop before trimming the excess wire.

six · Thread the beading needle with the beading thread. Pull half of the length through the needle to make a 24" (61cm) double strand of thread. Use the crimping pliers and a crimp bead to attach both thread ends to the eye pin loop (see "Using Crimp Beads," page 22).

seven · Randomly string assorted stone beads interspersed with small groupings of silver seed and "E" beads onto 14" (36cm) of the beading thread. To finish the beaded strand, string a crimp bead followed by enough silver seed beads to cover 1¼" (3cm) of the strand.

eight · Thread the needle through the top wire loop of the stone pendant that was set aside in step 3.

nine · To shape the loop of silver seed beads, thread the needle back up through the crimp bead and use the crimping pliers to squeeze the crimp bead flat. Trim the thread ends. The pendant should hang on a loop of beads. To fasten the necklace, fit the hook through the eye of the clasp.

one · String a small jasper bead onto a head pin, and then shape the wire with round-nose pliers. Thread the wire end through the bottom of the lock charm, and then wrap the wire end around itself twice before trimming.

Thread the suede through the bottom of an assembled pendant (see steps 1–2 on page 65 to make a pendant) and then through the key, lock and heart charms. Tie the suede ends in a square knot.

finished length: 18" (46cm)

LOCK AND KEY PENDANT CLASP

• SELECT YOUR FAVORITE CHARM AND POLISHED STONE TO HANG by the clasp. This necklace is customized by heart, lock and key charms. The length of the necklace is strung with a random mix of beads, making it an ideal catchall for leftover beads.

leather & rhinestone bracelet

MATERIALS

glass beads: purple, pink

crystal rhinestone bead

rhinestone heart charm

amethyst square pendant

light blue pony beads

lobster clasp

17" (43cm) of size 1mm round leather cord

finished length: 7½" (19cm)

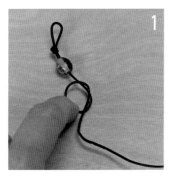

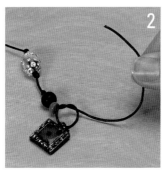

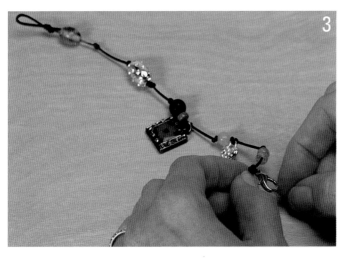

Irresistible flower pendants were the inspiration for this playful bracelet. The dark leather cord contrasts with the sparkling rhinestone beads, and the colored glass beads match the pendant to tie together the design. For another simply beautiful idea, see the variation on page 4.

one · Fold the leather end over and tie both thicknesses in an overhand knot to create a ½" (1cm) loop (see "Tying an Overhand Knot With a Loop," page 19). String one purple glass bead onto the leather. Then tie an overhand knot after the bead (see "Tying an Overhand Knot," page 18). The knots will position and space apart the beads on the cord.

two · Tie another overhand knot slightly away from the last knot in step 1. String a rhinestone bead then tie an overhand knot. Tie another knot slightly away from the last knot then string two purple glass beads, followed by the square pendant charm. Trap the charm in an overhand knot.

three · Tie an overhand knot slightly away from the pendant. String a pink glass bead followed by a rhinestone heart charm. Trap the charm in another overhand knot. Tie another knot slightly away from the charm; string two light blue pony beads. String the lobster clasp onto the leather end and secure by tying the end in a square knot (see "Tying a Square Knot," page 18). Trim the excess cord. To fasten the bracelet, simply hook the clasp through the leather loop.

shell anklets

MATERIALS

SHELL ANKLET

seed beads: violet, lilac

tan round glass beads

brown lip shell beads

two crimp tubes

spring clasp

11" (28cm) bead-stringing wire, .015" (.38mm) diameter

23½" (60cm) 32-gauge beading wire

crimping pliers

tape

finished length: 9" (23cm)

WHELK SHELL ANKLET
(page 71)

seed beads: pearl, purple

purple and brown glass beads

whelk shell beads

11" (28cm) bead-stringing wire, .015" (.38mm) diameter

23½" (60cm) 32-gauge beading wire

spring clasp

M aking these anklets (see page 71 for variation) is the perfect opportunity to explore the different varieties of seashells that have been transformed into beads. All are inexpensive and found in either the bead aisle or shell section of craft stores. Look for seed and glass beads that enhance the natural coloration of the shells.

Both anklets are made with two wires. The first is a strong stringing wire that contours the ankle and withstands friction. The second beading wire, which is not as strong but is more malleable, is perfect for threading through the shell beads while making the decorative teardrops.

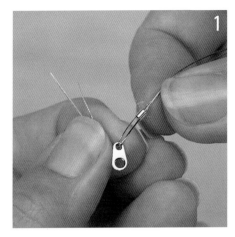

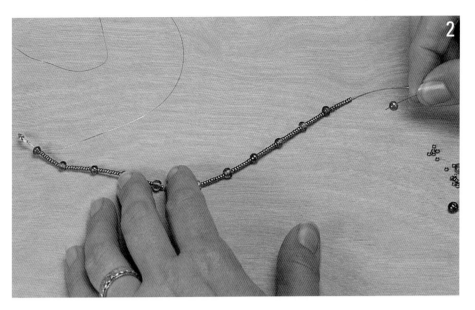

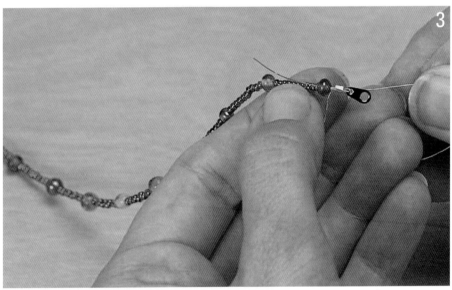

one • Thread one end of the stringing wire and one end of the beading wire together through a crimp tube and one part of the clasp, then back through the crimp tube. Use the crimping pliers to flatten the tube twice, trapping both ends in the compressions (see "Using Crimp Tubes," page 20).

two • Pull the beading wire to the side and string onto the stringing wire this bead sequence: one tan round glass bead and ten violet seed beads. Repeat the sequence to cover 8½" (22cm) of the wire (or enough length to wrap comfortably around your ankle). End with a round glass bead and tape off the end.

three • Thread the beading wire end through the first round glass bead on the stringing wire. Carefully pull the beading wire's length all the way through the bead (see "Preventing Twists in Wire," page 19).

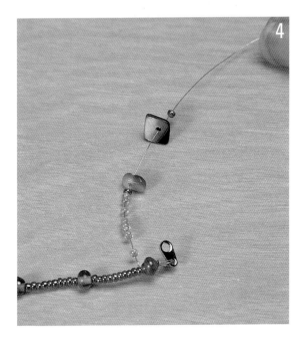

four • String onto the wire part one of the dangle beading sequence: eight lilac seed beads, one purple seed bead, two shell beads, and one purple seed bead.

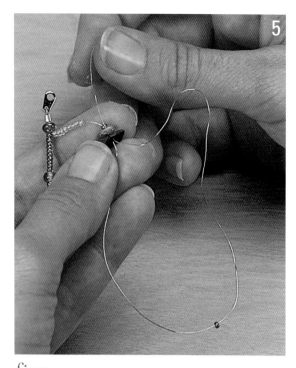

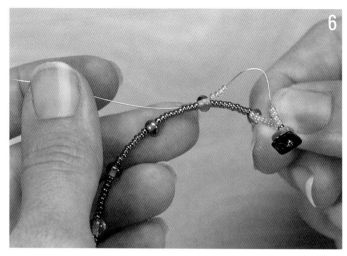

five · For part two of the dangle sequence, which shapes the dangle, thread the wire end back up through both shell beads and the first purple bead.

six · For part three of the dangle sequence, string eight lilac beads and then thread the wire through the next round glass bead on the stringing wire. Continue repeating the three parts of the dangle sequence to hang shells between all the round glass beads.

seven · After stringing the wire end through the last glass bead, thread both wires through a crimp tube and the other part of the clasp, then back through the crimp tube. Pull both ends tight before using crimping pliers to flatten the tube twice, trapping both ends in the compressions. Trim the wire ends.

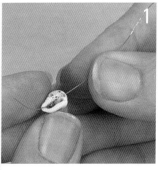

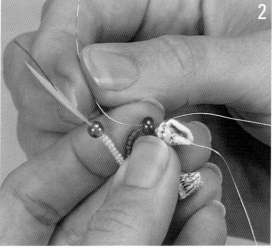

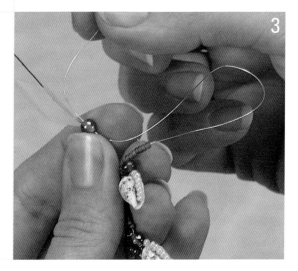

finished length: 9³/₄" (25cm)

WHELK SHELL ANKLET

• **I FOUND THESE INEXPENSIVE SHELLS** temporarily strung into necklaces to use for beach parties. This anklet's dangle is slightly different, as the wire that comes up from the base of the shell is camouflaged with seed beads.

one • Attach one part of the clasp to both the stringing and beading wires as in step 1, page 69. Thread the stringing wire as in step 2, page 69, substituting the following beading sequence: ten pearl seed beads and one purple round glass bead. Follow the dangle instructions in steps 3–6, pages 69–70, substituting the following dangle sequence for part one: seven purple seed beads and one brown glass bead. Bend the wire to thread it through the whelk shell (top to bottom).

two • For part two, string seven pearl seed beads onto the wire and then thread the wire back through the brown glass bead (the pearl seed beads will lay against the shell).

three • For part three of the dangle sequence, string seven purple seed beads onto the wire and then thread it through the next round glass bead on the stringing wire. Repeat the three parts of the dangle sequence to hang a whelk shell between all the purple round glass beads on the stringing wire. Attach the other part of the clasp to both wires as in step 7, page 70.

memory wire bracelets

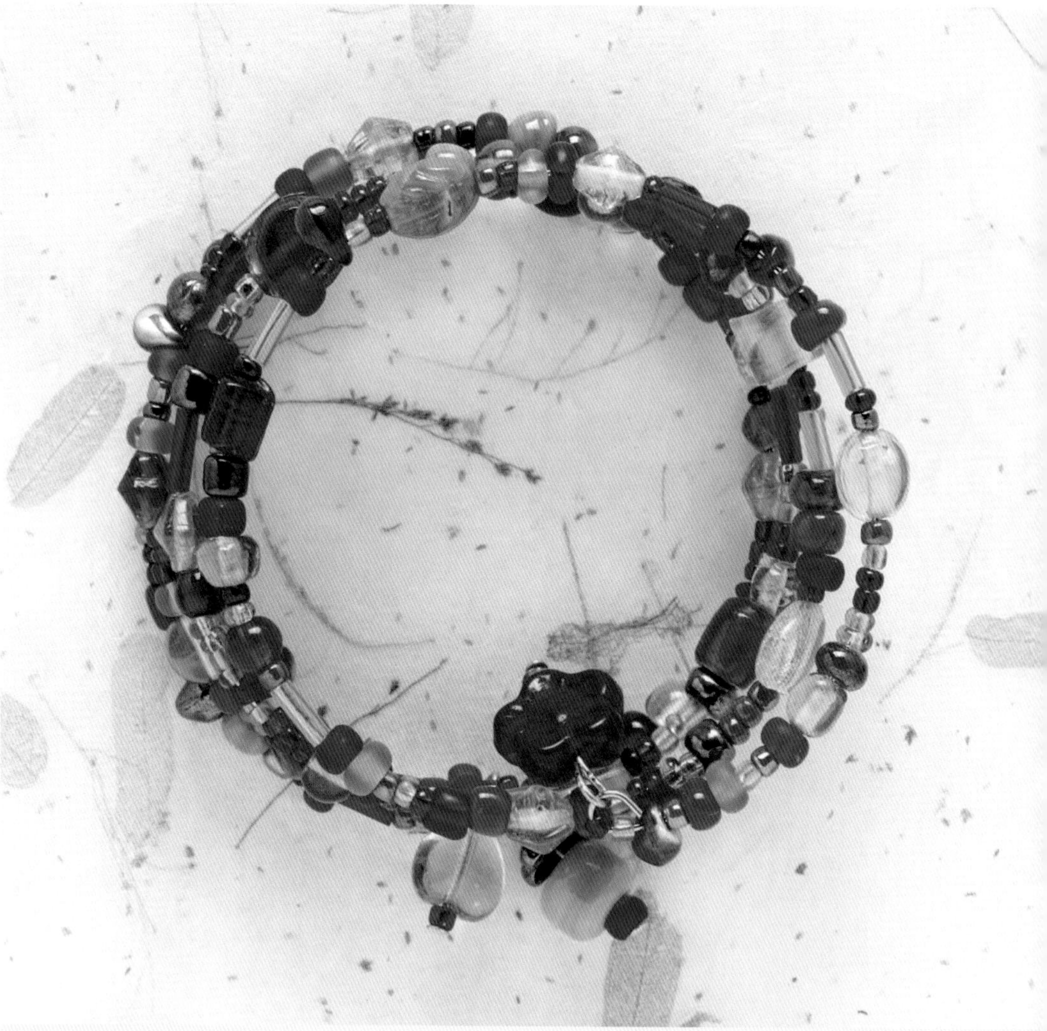

MATERIALS

assorted glass, seed and bugle beads

three 1" (3cm) head pins

memory wire (bracelet size)

wire cutters (or memory wire cutters)

round-nose pliers

Memory wire is fun to bead and wear. More resilient than a Slinky toy, the manufactured spiral shape is impossible to uncurl. To keep the bracelet easy and playful, I chose to randomly string assorted glass beads onto the wire. The looped wire ends serve two purposes: to secure the beads on the wire and to hold decorative bead charms.

MORE SIMPLY BEAUTIFUL IDEAS

To customize your bracelet, pull together a mix of various-sized beads in a light to dark range of your favorite color. Set apart your favorite larger beads and turn them into charms to hang from the beaded bracelet end loops.

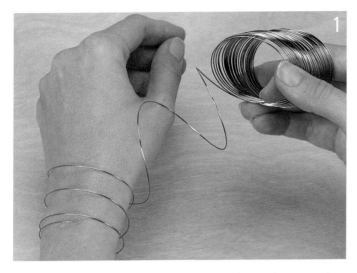

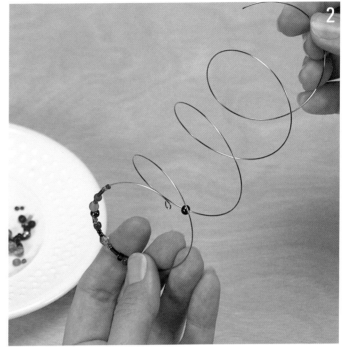

one · Wrap the memory wire around your wrist to gauge the necessary length. (I find a half turn followed by three full turns and another half turn to be a desirable length.) Mark the spot with your fingertips and remove the bracelet from your wrist. Cut the measured memory wire with wire cutters.

two · Use round-nose pliers to bend one end of the memory wire into a loop (see "Looping Wire Ends," page 23). Randomly string assorted glass, seed and bugle beads onto the other end of the wire.

three · Once you've completely filled the wire with beads, use the round-nose pliers to turn the second wire end over into a loop.

four · String one to two beads onto each of the three head pins (see "Shaping Head Pins," page 25). Then, thread one of the beaded pins through the loop created in step 2. Use round-nose pliers to bend the pin end over to secure it to the bracelet. Repeat the process to attach a second beaded head pin to the same loop. Thread the third head pin onto the loop created in step 3.

double-strand bracelets

MATERIALS

BRACELET

red 8mm glass bead

seed beads: metallic red and silver

silver "E" beads

red "E" beads

red flat glass beads

72" (183cm) of 32-gauge beading wire

finished length: 8" (20cm)

RING
(page 77)

seed beads (two silver, then enough metallic red to wrap beaded length around finger)

flat glass bead

10" (25cm) of 32-gauge beading wire

At first glance, these intricate bracelets appear complicated to bead, but they're not. Each center grouping of beads is strung onto two wires, and the side beads are strung onto a single wire. This simple pattern repeats for the entire length of the bracelet. Seed and "E" beads complement the center glass beads, making this bracelet a bargain to assemble.

MORE SIMPLY BEAUTIFUL IDEAS

Any uniform glass beads can be worked into this technique. I'd suggest low-profile beads that will lie flat around the wrist. The length of the bead will in part determine the width of the bracelet, as the beads are strung sideways. A small single strand of temporarily strung beads is the perfect quantity of beads for this project. The understated gray and silver bracelet (shown below) is assembled with a single hematite tube bead in the center and a single silver seed bead on each side. Use a 7.5 round hematite bead for the clasp. Finished lengths: 8" (20cm)

one · Fold a 72" (183cm) length of beading wire in half. String twenty-one metallic red seed beads onto one end of the wire and slide them down to the center fold, placing 10 beads on one side and 11 beads on the other. Thread both wire ends through a silver "E" bead to cap the loop portion of the clasp. An 8mm glass bead will need to fit through the loop in order for the clasp to work. If necessary, remove the "E" bead and add or delete seed beads in the loop. Replace the "E" bead after any such adjustments.

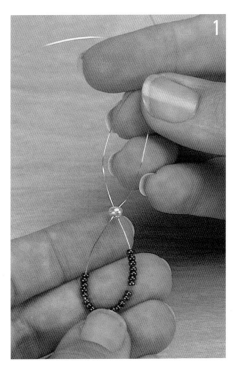

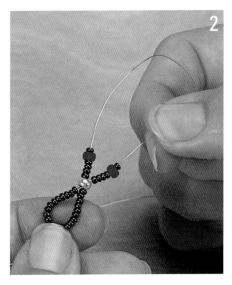

two · String onto each strand four metallic red seed beads, one red "E" bead and one metallic red seed bead.

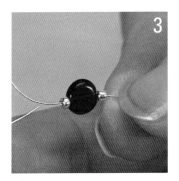

three · String one silver seed bead, one red flat glass bead and one silver seed bead onto one of the wires. Thread the second wire through those three beads in the opposite direction.

four · Hold one wire in each hand and use even pressure to pull the wires out from the bracelet (see "Preventing Twists in Wire," page 19). This will slide the beads down.

five · String onto each strand one metallic red seed bead, one red "E" bead and one metallic red seed bead.

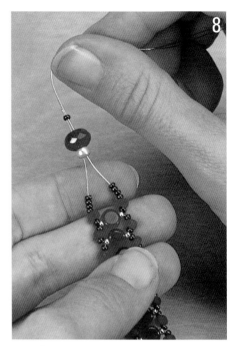

six · Repeat steps 3–5, ending with step 3, until you have 6" (15cm) of beaded length.

seven · String onto each strand one metallic red seed bead, one red "E" bead and four metallic red seed beads.

eight · Bring both wires together and thread them through one silver "E" bead, one red 8mm glass bead and one metallic red seed bead.

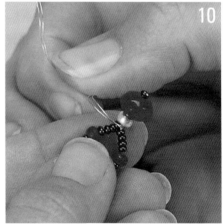

nine · Thread both wire ends back down through the red glass bead and silver "E" bead. Do not go back through the red metallic seed bead; it holds the red 8mm glass bead in place.

ten · Tightly wrap the two wires several times under the silver "E" bead before trimming away the excess wire.

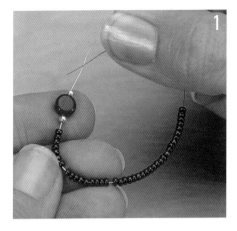

DOUBLE-STRAND RINGS

• THIS LITTLE RING IS THE PERFECT COMPLEMENT

to the double-strand bracelet and can probably be assem-

bled with leftover beads. Even if you're not interested in

completing a matching set, this ring is the perfect way to

showcase a single bead.

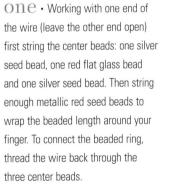

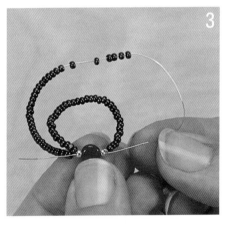

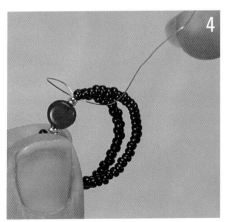

one • Working with one end of the wire (leave the other end open) first string the center beads: one silver seed bead, one red flat glass bead and one silver seed bead. Then string enough metallic red seed beads to wrap the beaded length around your finger. To connect the beaded ring, thread the wire back through the three center beads.

two • Wrap the emerging wire end three times around the ring band wire alongside the silver seed bead and then trim the wire end.

three • String enough metallic red seed beads onto the remaining wire end to create a second ring band equal in length to the first ring band. To connect the second ring band, thread the wire end back through the center beads.

four • Wrap the second wire three times around the ring band wire alongside the silver seed bead and then trim the excess wire.

crystal bubble rings

MATERIALS

iridescent 6mm crystal bead

five sapphire 4mm round crystal beads

seed beads

iridescent 8mm sequin cups

18" (46cm) of 32-gauge beading wire

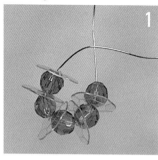

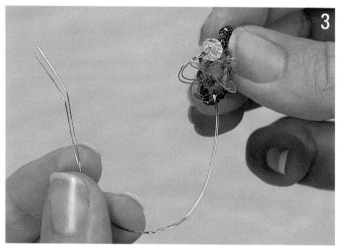

I riridescent, inexpensive and fun, these costume jewelry rings are conversation starters. Make them in an array of colors as special gifts for friends who are young at heart.

one · String a sequin cup followed by a 4mm round crystal bead onto one end of the wire, and repeat this sequence four times. Slide the five sequin cups and five beads onto the center of the wire. Bring both sides of the wire together above the sequin cups and beads to form a flower shape, and twist the wires together.

two · String seed beads onto both wires until you have enough beaded length to wrap around your finger. Pull the wire ends up through the center of the flower shape. Wrap the wires once around the outside of the flower shape to attach the beaded ring band to the other side of the flower.

three · Thread the wire ends back up through the center of the flower shape and through a 6mm iridescent crystal bead. Thread both wires back down through the center of the flower shape. Wrap the wires twice around the other side of the flower shape. Trim the excess wire.

toe rings

MATERIALS

10mm floral spacer
(low-profile or flat beads work best)

6" (15cm) of .5mm clear stretch
beading elastic (such as transparent
Stretchy Illusion cord)

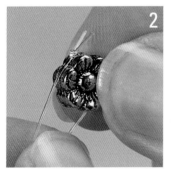

one · Thread one end of the elastic through spacer. Fit the spacer over the toe, bringing the elastic ends together to approximate the size of the loop needed. Bring both ends together and tie them in an overhand knot (see "Tying an Overhand Knot," page 18). Pull the knot tight and trim the ends.

two · Slide the knot inside the bead so that the knot is completely concealed.

These toe rings take only a minute to make and are a must-have summer accessory. There's a wide array of inexpensive metal flower spacer beads to choose from, so the toe rings can have a variety of looks. Unlike traditional toe rings, an invisible strand of elastic custom fits around the toe.

accessories

Surround yourself with beautiful beads all day long. They'll bring you pleasure when you grab your keys, glance at your watch, mark your page or even tie back your hair. Original and practical, these accessories are perfect for people with active lifestyles.

Coordinate the beads with your favorite clothes, shoes, handbags and eyeglasses to create accessories that complement your style from head to toe. Designed to withstand everyday wear, all the beads in these projects are securely wired, glued, sewn or knotted in place.

Simple and inexpensive, many of these accessory projects make ideal gifts. With just a little practice you can quickly assemble them. A handmade gift is always meaningful, especially if the design is custom made. Share the simple joys of beading with your family and friends.

CHAPTER

2

double-banded watches

MATERIALS

6mm semiprecious turquoise bead

8mm semiprecious turquoise bead

turquoise stone chips

red coral beads

silver spacer beads

black glass beads: butterfly, round, oval

two 2-hole spacer bars

daisy toggle clasp

two crimp tubes

watch face

two 18" (46cm) strands of Soft Flex, nylon-coated stainless steel beading wire, .014" (36mm) diameter

crimping pliers

finished length:
7¼" (18cm)

ANOTHER SIMPLY BEAUTIFUL IDEA

Combine shaped glass, semiprecious stone and silver spacer beads to make these intriguing watch straps. Two-hole spacer bars hold the two bands of beads together. Select an ornate clasp that complements both the watch face and the beads. If you prefer a more casual look, substitute a continuous length of heavyweight clear elastic for the two lengths of beading wire and the clasp.

Pair semiprecious turquoise beads, amber glass beads and silver beads to create this south-western-inspired watchstrap. Both watch bands have limited color combinations; the variety is in the shape and size of the individual beads. Finished length: 7½" (19cm)

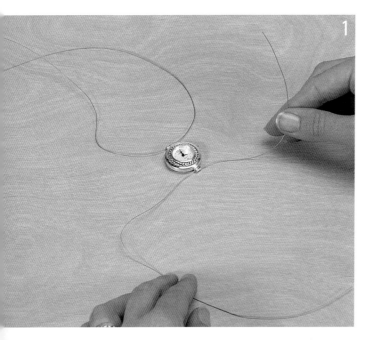

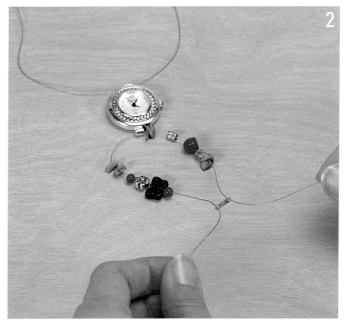

one · Thread one 18" (46cm) length of beading wire into the opening at the top of the watch face. Pull 9" 23cm) of the wire through the opening so that the length is folded in half. Repeat with one 18" (46cm) length of beading wire at the base of the watch face.

two · Working from the base of the watch face, begin stringing turquoise stone chips onto each wire. Continue beading, switching to a mix of black glass, coral and silver spacer beads until the beading measures 1" (3cm) in length. Next, thread each wire through a hole in the spacer bar. Resume beading until the total beaded length is 2⅝" (7cm). Adjust this measurement as necessary to work with both your wrist size and the size of the clasp.

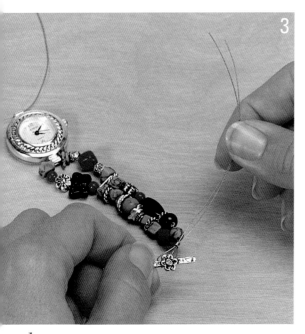

three · Thread both wires through a crimp tube and one side of the clasp and then back through the crimp tube. Pull the wires tight, then crimp the tube twice using crimping pliers (see "Using Crimp Tubes," page 20). Trim the two wire ends.

four · Repeat steps 2 and 3 to bead the other side of the band, starting from the top of the watch face.

key chain

MATERIALS

one to two millefiori (or multichip) glass beads

one to two large opaque glass beads

32mm split ring

16½" (42cm) black leather cord

one · Fold the leather in half and thread both ends up through the center of the split ring. Thread the ends through the middle of the center fold, and then pull them tight so that the resulting knot rests against the split ring.

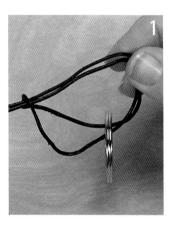

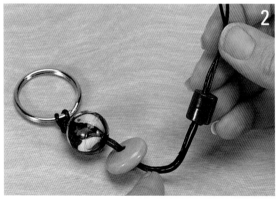

Millefiori glass beads are the focal point of this elegant key chain. Their heavy weight feels good in the palm of the hand, and the bright bursts of colors will help prevent keys from being misplaced.

two · Thread both leather ends through two or three glass beads. (I used one millefiori bead, one yellow donut bead and one blue tube bead.)

three · Hold both cords together and tie an overhand knot (see "Tying an Overhand Knot," page 18). Slide the knot right up under the last bead before pulling it tight. Then tie a single overhand knot at the end of each cord.

eyeglasses chain

MATERIALS

black twisted bugle beads

silver seed beads

silver "E" beads

cube (square) beads

two crimp tubes

two eyeglass holder loops

30" (76cm) bead-stringing wire, nylon-coated stainless steel, .012" (.31mm) diameter

crimping pliers

finished length: 29³/₄" (76cm)

one · Use the crimping pliers and a crimp tube to attach one end of the wire to one end of an eyeglass holder (see "Using Crimp Tubes," page 20). String one silver seed bead onto the wire. Next, string the following bead sequence: five black twisted bugle beads, one silver seed bead, one silver "E" bead and one silver seed bead.

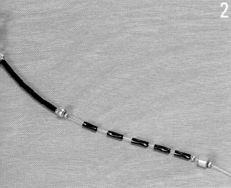

I keenly realized the necessity of this accessory when I watched my only pair of glasses sink out of reach into a lake. Made with basic black bugle beads and silver accents, this chain is a stylish way to keep your specs handy and avoid unfortunate mishaps.

two · Repeat the sequence, but use one cube bead instead of one silver "E" bead. Repeat the bead sequence fifteen times, alternately using one silver "E" bead or one cube bead in each sequence.

three · After the last bead sequence, string five black twisted bugle beads and one silver seed bead onto the wire. Use the crimping pliers and a crimp tube to attach one end of the other eyeglass holder to the end of the wire.

stretch bookmarks

MATERIALS

assorted glass beads (I suggest using
flat or low-profile bead varieties)

two crimps (each with two extended
sides that fold over the cord)

5¼" x 8½" (13cm x 22cm)
blank book or journal

17" (43cm) of size 1mm stretch beading
elastic (such as Stretch Magic)

needle-nose pliers

awl

Turn a simple journal into a beautiful beaded accessory. The stretchy length of beads is not just for looks; it pulls over the front cover to hold the book closed or inside the book to mark a page. Look for simple journals, covered with handmade papers, that will complement the beads.

ANOTHER SIMPLY
BEAUTIFUL
IDEA

For this journal, I took color cues from the handmade paper covering. The turquoise, purple and white pressed glass beads pick up shades in the paper fibers. I also chose to string the beads in a repetitive leaf and flower pattern, spacing each shaped bead with a simple small pearl bead.

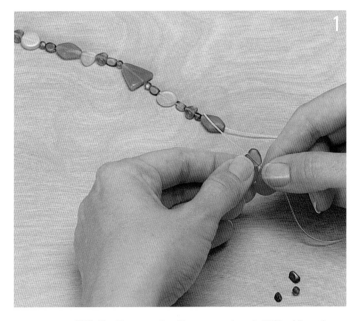

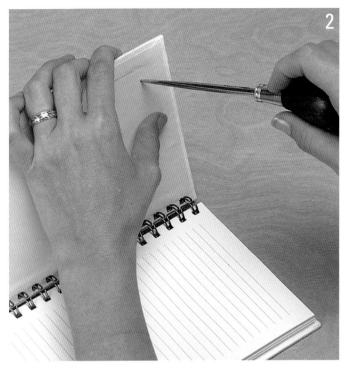

one • Tie an overhand knot approximately 3" (8cm) from the end of the stretch elastic (see "Tying an Overhand Knot," page 18). String assorted glass beads onto 8½" (22cm) of the elastic. (If your book or journal is a different size, string enough beads to span the height of the book.) Tie an overhand knot above the last bead.

two • Use an awl to make two holes in the back cover of the journal. Position the first hole 1" (3cm) down from the top edge of the book and 1" (3cm) from the right edge. Position the second hole 1" (3cm) up from the bottom edge and 1" (3cm) from the right edge.

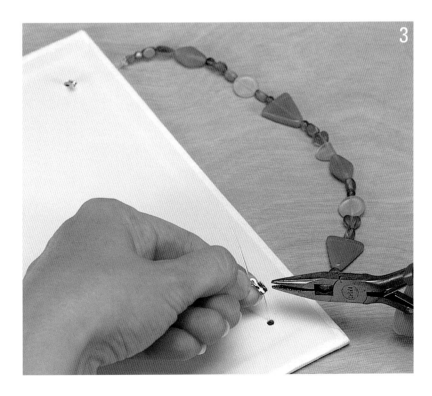

three • Thread one end of the elastic from the outside in through a punched hole in the back of the journal. Working on the inside of the back cover, pull ½" (1cm) of the elastic through the hole in a crimp. Leave 1½" (4cm) of elastic between the knot and the crimp. Use pliers to fold one side of the crimp down over the elastic, and then fold the second side over the first. Trim the excess elastic. Repeat the process to attach the other end of the elastic through the second hole.

bead-dazzled photo album

MATERIALS

round and flower-shaped sequins

seed beads

¼ yard (23cm) of cotton fabric
(standard width)

6½" x 14½" (17cm x 37cm) fusible
web for light- to midweight fabrics

6¼" x 6½" (16cm x 17cm) two-ring photo
album (bound album will not work)

black sewing thread (or a color to match
or coordinate with of the beads)

size 10 beading needle

double-sided craft tape, ¼" (6mm)
and ½" (1cm) widths

iron

Transform an inexpensive photo album into a special keepsake. Pair colorful seed beads and sequins and sew them onto playful printed cotton. Simply wrap the resulting eye-catching fabric around the album and hold it in place with craft tape.

tip > If you are using a different-sized photo album, figure an extra 1" (3cm) each for the top and bottom and 1½" (4cm) each for the sides.

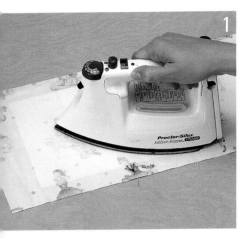

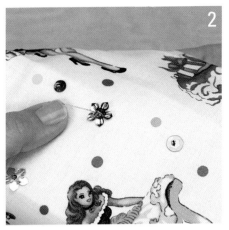

one · Center the fusible web on the wrong side of the fabric, and then iron it in place.

two · Thread the needle and knot the end of the sewing thread. Bring the needle up through the back of the fabric and through one sequin and one seed bead.

three · Bring the needle back through the sequin and the fabric. Repeat the process begun in step 2 to distribute beads and sequins over the front of the fabric.

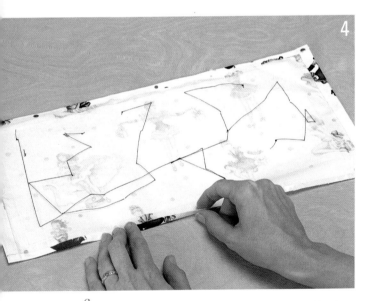

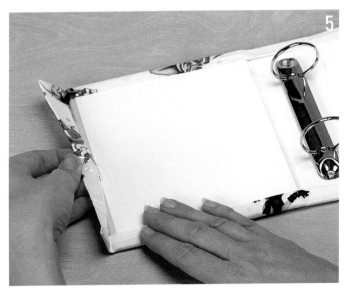

four · Apply one strip of double-sided craft tape (½" [1cm] wide) to each side edge of the fabric. Next peel the film off the tape and fold the fabric in onto itself. Repeat the process with the top and bottom fabric edges, using the ¼" (6mm) tape.

*tip > Folded fabric may become bulky at the corners. To ensure that the fabric will lie flat, snip a triangle off the folded fabric from under each corner of the album before taping the fabric down.

five · Remove the album pages and the album cover's plastic wrapping. Position the album over the wrong side of the fabric, centering it over the fusible web. Place a long strip of double-sided craft tape (¼" [6mm] wide) across the top edge of the fabric. Peel the film off the tape, and then fold the tape-covered fabric edge over the top the album. Repeat the process for the bottom edge of the album. Apply double-sided craft tape (½" [1cm] wide) along the inside edge of the fabric on each side of the album. Fold the sides of the fabric over the album and then press them down. Insert the album pages.

wire leaf bookmarks

MATERIALS

three assorted glass beads with narrow holes (so they don't slide over the bottom of the head pin)

2" (5cm) gold head pin

22-gauge colored wire (I used Fun Wire)

needle-nose pliers

round-nose pliers

leaf pattern (page 126)

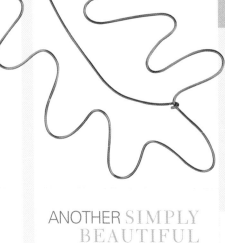

Turn over a new leaf without losing the page you're on. A piece of jewelry for your books, this clever leaf lays flat between the pages while the stem dangles beads over the spine. This project is easier than it looks; the malleable wire simply gets bent around the pattern on page 126 to create a leaf.

ANOTHER SIMPLY BEAUTIFUL IDEA

Shaped with copper-colored wire, the oak leaf is constructed just like the green leaf. Pair donut and oval-shaped beads together to create an imitation acorn bead dangle.

90

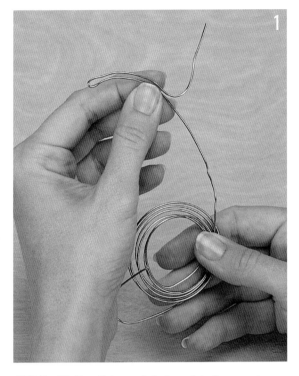

two · Shape the leaf using the pattern on page 126 as a reference. Use your fingertips to bend the wire back and forth to create the bumpy leaf edge.

one · Working off the spool of wire and starting a couple inches from the wire end, fold one loop for the stem of the leaf.

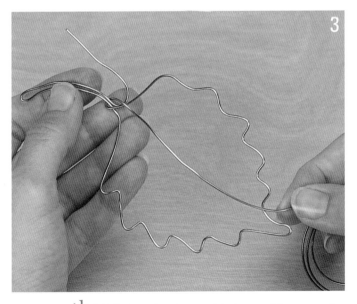

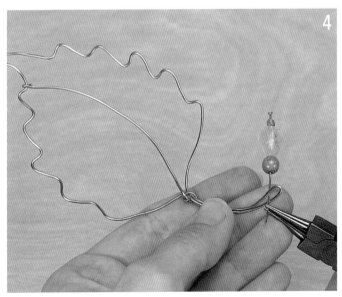

three · Loop the wire around the bottom of the stem, and then bring the wire down the center of the leaf. Wrap the wire once around the bottom of the leaf and cut off the excess wire. Wrap the starting wire end once around the top of the leaf, and then trim the excess. Squeeze both wrapped ends flat with needle-nose pliers.

four · Starting with the smallest bead, slide three beads onto the head pin. Thread the wire pin end through the loop in the stem. Use round-nose pliers to fold the end over so that it rests against itself. The connected bead dangle should swing freely.

beaded boxes

MATERIALS

tiny glass marbles

black glass bead

gold and black ceramic bead

4" (diameter) x 2½" (height) (10cm x 6cm) colored oval papier mâché box

2½" x 12" (6cm x 30cm) piece of scrapbook paper

15" (38cm) of ⅝" (2cm) wide ribbon

12" (30cm) elastic beading cord

5" (13cm) of 26-gauge wire

double-sided adhesive

glue stick

glue gun

awl

The lid of the bead-clasp box is covered with tiny shimmering marbles that are held in place invisibly by a sheet of double-sided adhesive. The decorative paper and grosgrain ribbon set off the ornate bead clasp. This elegant little box is a perfect gift in and of itself; for a real surprise, tuck a handmade beaded necklace inside.

ANOTHER SIMPLY BEAUTIFUL IDEA

Take advantage of paper boxes manufactured in bright colors that shine through clear marbles on the lid. This box is embellished with black, red and gold decorative paper, clear tiny marbles, black braided trim, black and gold ceramic beads and a clear glass bead. (The box shown above is 3" (8cm) in diameter and 2¼" (6cm) tall.)

one · Trace the box lid onto a sheet of double-sided adhesive. Cut out the oval, and then peel one side of the backing off the adhesive. Apply the exposed adhesive to the top of the lid and remove the other side of the backing. To apply the marbles, place the lid on a plate and pour the marbles onto the adhesive, or pour the marbles directly into the plate first and then press the inverted lid into the marbles.

two · Use hot glue to attach the ribbon around the edge of the lid. Line up the top edge of the ribbon with the tops of the marbles on the lid to help keep them in place.

three · Apply glue stick to the back of the scrapbook paper, and then wrap the paper around the sides of the box.

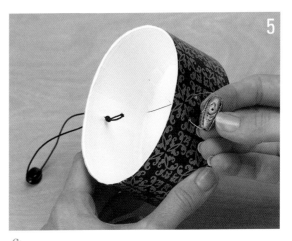

four · Use an awl to punch a hole in the center back of the box below the lid, about ¾" (2cm) from the top edge of the box. String the black glass bead onto the center of the elastic beading cord, and then thread both ends of the cord through the hole. Hold the ends together and tie an overhand knot inside the box (see "Tying an Overhand Knot," page 18).

five · Punch two holes centered on the front of the box and ¾" (2cm) from the top of the box. The distance between the holes will depend on the width of the bead you use. String a gold and black ceramic bead onto the center of a 5" (13cm) piece of wire. Thread the wire ends through the holes in the front of the box and then twist the wires together inside the box. Replace the lid. Stretch the elastic loop over the lid and hook the black bead under the gold and black ceramic bead.

beaded frame

MATERIALS

green glass mosaic beads

2" x 2" (5cm x 5cm) frame

jewelry glue or Aleene's Platinum Bond
Glass & Bead Slick Surfaces Adhesive

straight pin

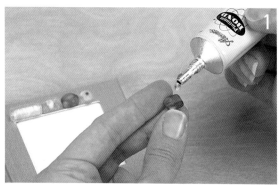

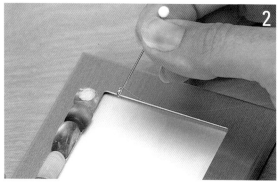

The mosaic and tiling craft trend has prompted glass bead manufacturers to create flat-backed (half) beads. They're sold grouped by color in mixed-variety packs. Simple silver frames complement the inherent size, tone and pattern variations of these hand-made beads.

one · Arrange the beads around the opening of the frame, distributing varieties and colors evenly among each of the four sides. Once you're pleased with the arrangement, carefully set the four rows of beads aside. Working with one row of beads and one side of the frame at a time, apply a small amount of glue to the back of each bead.

two · Glue beads to each side of the frame. Sometimes glue will come out from under the sides of the beads. Use the tip of a straight pin to remove excess glue.

three · If necessary, before the glue dries, make slight adjustments to the beads' positioning so that the rows meet at the corners.

ponytail holder

MATERIALS

antique silver metal bead

silver foil bead

elastic hair bands

4" (10cm) of 32-gauge beading wire

jewelry glue or Aleene's Platinum Bond
Glass & Bead Slick Surfaces Adhesive

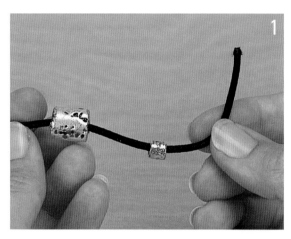

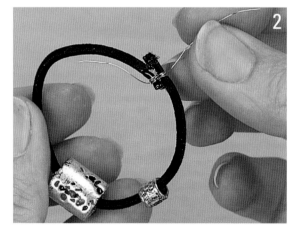

If you often reach for an elastic band to pull your hair back, you'll appreciate the simple elegance of this everyday accessory. Select beads with wide openings and colors that match your favorite clothes to create ponytail holders that coordinate with your personal style.

one • Cut one elastic hair band apart where it was glued together in manufacturing. String one foil bead and one antique silver bead onto the elastic. NOTE: The beads for this project need to have holes wide enough to accommodate the elastic.

two • Place a small amount of glue on one end of the elastic, and then overlap that end over the other end. Tightly wrap the two ends together with beading wire.

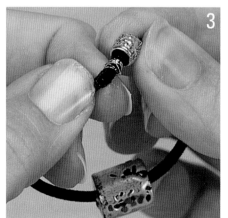

three • Apply more glue around the wrapped wire and elastic ends. Slip the antique silver bead over the wet glue to conceal the wrapped connection. Allow the glue to dry completely before wearing the beaded ponytail holder.

twisted-wire headband

MATERIALS

freshwater pearls

glass leaf beads, each with
a hole at the base

large elastic hair band

76" (193cm) of 26-gauge wire

Crown your hair with a twisted-wire stem that's budding with pearls and glass leaf beads. The wired beads hold the hair out of the face, and also prevent the headband from slipping. Only seconds to pull over your head, it's a practical hairstyling solution.

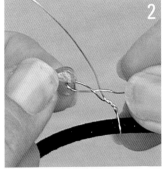

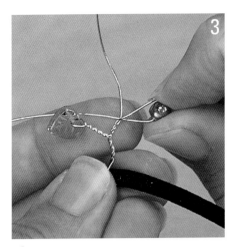

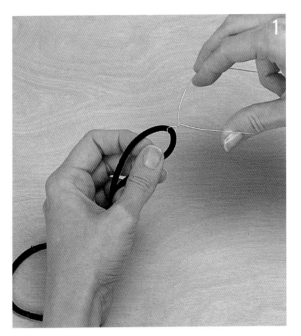

two · String a leaf bead onto the first wire. Slide the bead down the wire and position it ½" (1cm) from the twist. Fold the wire back (toward the headband) and hold the bead while you twist the first wire three times. Then twist both wires together three times.

three · String one pearl onto the second wire, and position it ½" (1cm) from the twist. Fold the wire back and twist it three times. Twist the two wires together three times.

one · Loop the center of 72" (183cm) of wire around the hair band. Twist the wire together three times to make two equal lengths of wire connected to the hair band (see "Twisting Wire," page 23).

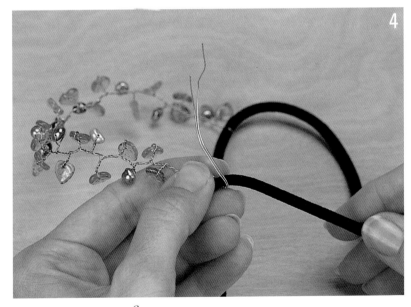

four · Repeat steps 2 and 3 until you have 9" (23cm) of beading. Loop the two wires together through the hair band at the point opposite that in step 1. Twist them back around the end of the twisted headband two to three times before trimming the ends.

five · Shape the hair band into a figure eight by tightly wrapping a 4" (10cm) piece of wire around the middle of the hair band. Trim the wire ends and fold them down between the two thicknesses of elastic.

wired-pearl barrettes

MATERIALS

BARRETTES

8mm pearlized glass beads:
silver, white, pink

8mm patina pearls: purple, coral

silver leaf beads

2¼" (6cm) barrettes

15" (38cm) of 20-gauge wire (per barrette)

wire cutters

needle-nose pliers

HAIR PICKS
(page 100)

two purple 8mm patina pearls

two green 13mm x 11mm patina pearls

two silver leaf beads

two hair picks

10" (25cm) of 20-gauge wire (per pick)

jewelry glue or Aleene's Platinum Bond
Glass & Bead Slick Surfaces Adhesive

round-nose pliers

HAIR PINS
(page 101)

rice pink pearls (or semiprecious pearls)

two silver leaf beads

two bobby pins

12" (30cm) of 20-gauge wire (per bobby pin)

Simple black wire and barrettes are the perfect backdrop for colored-glass pearl beads accented with silver leaf beads. Not only beautiful, these barrettes are wired to withstand everyday wear.

ANOTHER SIMPLY
BEAUTIFUL
IDEA

Bead larger barrettes perfect for thick ponytails. Start with a 3½" (9cm) barrette, and alternately wire a pair of 8mm beads with a single 13mm x 11mm patina pearl. Incorporate six silver leaf beads between and on the sides of the 8mm bead pairs.

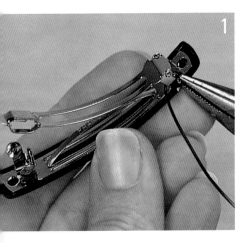

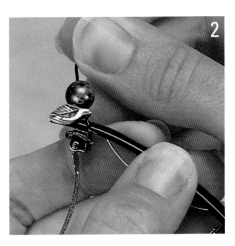

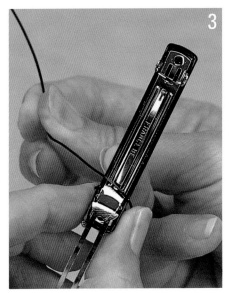

one · Wrap the wire end once around one side of the hinged post on the barrette back. Use needle-nose pliers to flatten the wire end flat against the post.

two · String one leaf and one pearl bead onto the end of the wire, and then wrap the wire around the top of the barrette.

three · Pull the wire tight so there is no slack in the wire and the pearl lies flat against the barrette.

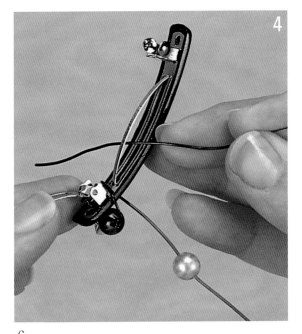

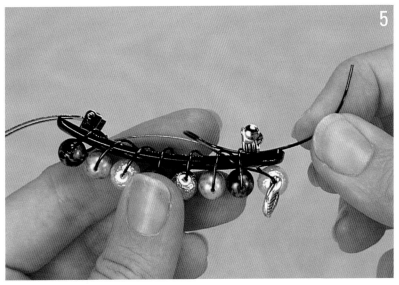

four · Add one pearl and wrap the wire around the top of the barrette. Thread the wire under the spring bar so that you don't interfere with the clasp's function.

five · Continue stringing single pearls and wrapping the wire until you've wired seven pearls to the top of the barrette. String one pearl bead followed by one leaf bead onto the wire. Wrap the wire around the top of the barrette. Continue wrapping the wire around the barrette before securing the end around one post of the clasp. Use wire cutters to trim the excess wire, and use needle-nose pliers to flatten the wire end against the post.

HAIR PICKS

• SIMPLY ELEGANT HAIR

picks anchor twisted topknot

hairstyles in place. Wire wraps

pearls and a metal leaf bead

around a purchased hair pick,

so this project takes only min-

utes to make.

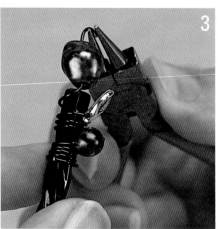

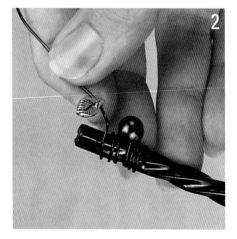

one · Start wrapping the wire ¾" (2cm) from the top of one hair pick. Wrap it about four times before string-ing an 8mm purple patina pearl bead onto the wire end.

two · Wrap the wire around the pick two more times, and then string a leaf bead.

three · Wrap the wire around the pick one more time before string-ing the 13mm x 11mm pearl onto the wire. If necessary, trim the wire end so that there's ¼" (6mm) of wire left to loop with round-nose pliers (see "Looping Wire Ends," page 23). Add a drop of glue to the underside of the pearl to better secure it to the top of the pick. Add a drop of glue under the leaf end to anchor it upright against the base of the large pearl. Repeat steps 1–3 for the second hair pick.

HAIR PINS

• SUBTLE PEARL-COVERED BOBBY

pins offer a pretty way to hold stray

locks in place.

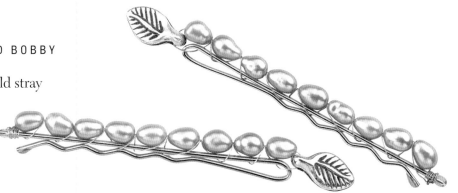

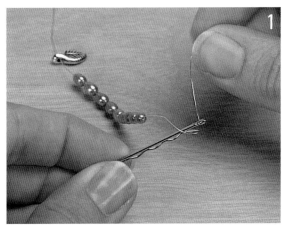

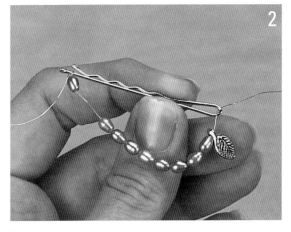

one • String one leaf bead and nine pearls onto the wire. Wrap the pearl end of the wire four times around the tip of the flat side of the pin.

two • Thread the other end of the wire through the loop in the bobby pin.

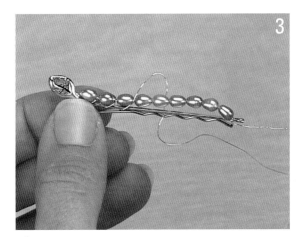

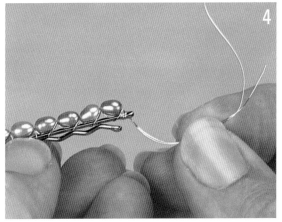

three • Holding the leaf bead, work your way down the length of the bobby pin and wrap the wire between each bead and under the bobby pin's flat side. Be sure you don't wire the bobby pin closed; slide the wire between the flat and bumpy sides of the bobby pin with each wrap.

four • Once you've secured all the beads, twist the two wire ends together. Then wrap the connected wires one time around the tip of the bobby pin before trimming the ends.

people pins

MATERIALS

PEOPLE PINS

19mm bugle beads (for legs)

6mm circle beads (for feet)

13mm bugle beads (for arms)

two pink bicone beads (for hands)

13mm resin bead (head);
select a bead that can accommodate
four thicknesses of wire

two 10mm pink faceted beads (for skirt)

pink ceramic heart bead (for bodice)

½" (1cm) two-hole pin back

light pink and dark pink 24-gauge wire:
two 4¾" (12cm) pieces (for arms)
and two 6¼" (16cm) pieces (for legs)

jewelry glue or Aleene's Platinum Bond
Glass & Bead Slick Surfaces Adhesive

round-nose pliers

small screwdriver

PEOPLE & POOCH PIN
(page 104)

four 13mm bugle beads (for legs)

four bronze donut beads (for feet)

amber resin bead (for body);
select a bead that can accommodate
four thicknesses of wire

large oval bead (for head)

amber glass bead (for neck)

white donut beads (for chest)

teardrop-shaped bead (for tail)

two medium oval beads (for ears)

black seed bead (for nose)

½" (1cm) two-hole pin back

24-gauge gold wire: two 3" (8cm) pieces
(for legs), 6½" (17cm) piece (for tail),
2" (5cm) piece (for nose and head)

materials to make one people pin

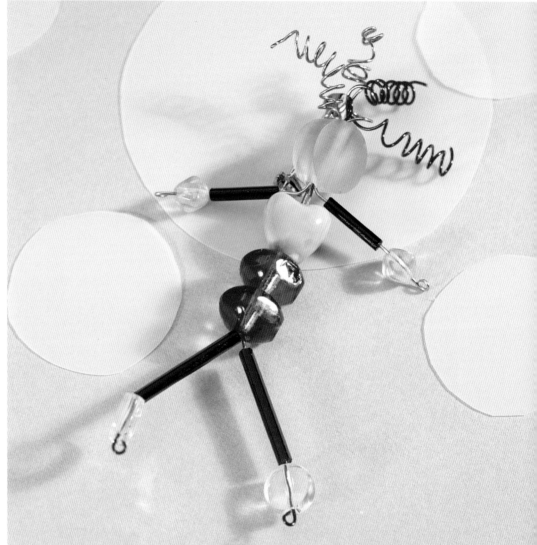

These people pins are just plain fun! The arms and legs are made from long bugle beads. The head, hands and feet are low-profile round beads that lie flat against clothing. Go wild with the body beads and wire colors to create new beaded fashions.

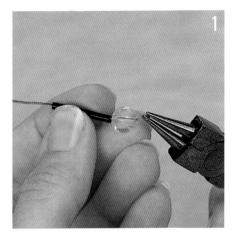

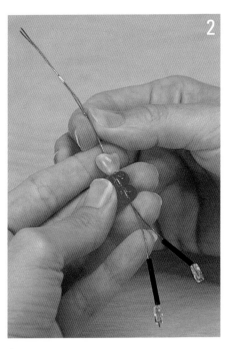

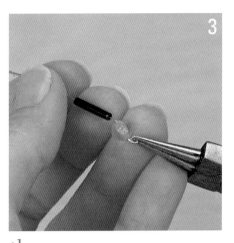

one · Begin making the feet and legs by string-ing one 6mm circle bead and one 19mm bugle bead onto each 6¼" (16cm) length of wire. Use round-nose pliers to loop the wire end under each foot to prevent the beads from sliding off (see "Looping Wire Ends," page 23).

two · Bring the tops of the leg wires together and thread them through the two faceted beads and the ceramic heart bead.

three · String one bicone and one 13mm bugle bead onto each 4¾" (12cm) length of wire. Use round-nose pliers to loop the wire under each hand.

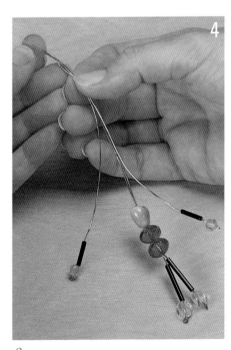

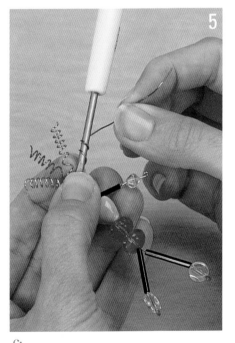

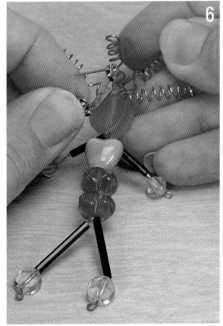

four · Bring the tops of the arm and leg wires together and thread them all through the 13mm resin bead. Slide the resin bead down the wires so it rests above the top of the arm and bodice beads.

five · Position a small screwdriver (or nail) on top of the head and spiral one wire end up the shaft to shape a lock of hair. Slide the screwdriver out of the coiled wire, and repeat the process with the remain-ing three wires.

six · Glue the pin back to a flat bead. In the pin shown, the pin back is glued to the back of the head. Allow the glue to dry overnight before wearing the pin.

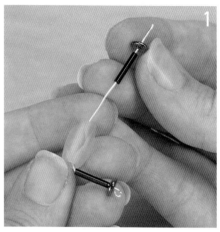

one · Thread the center of one 3" (8cm) leg wire through the amber resin bead. String one 13mm bugle bead followed by one bronze donut bead onto each end of the wire. Use round-nose pliers to loop the wire ends under each foot (see "Looping Wire Ends," page 23).

PEOPLE & POOCH PIN

• THIS PET-FRIENDLY PEOPLE PIN WILL walk her dog all day long and not get very far pinned to your jacket. Make a people pin, and then make a dog pin as well. Join the two together by looping a small length of wire around the person's hand and the dog's neck. Be sure to secure both pins to your clothing as the wire leash alone will not support the dog's weight.

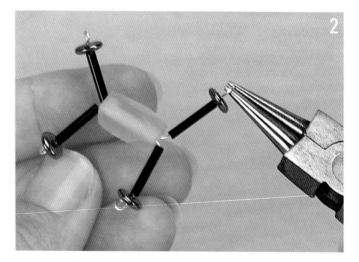

two · Repeat step 1 to add a second pair of legs and feet to the body.

three · String the teardrop-shaped bead onto the center of the 6½" (17cm) wire. Fold the wire in half, trapping the end of the bead in the fold. Thread both wire ends through the resin bead.

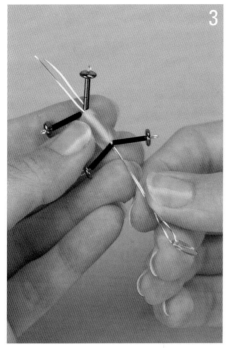

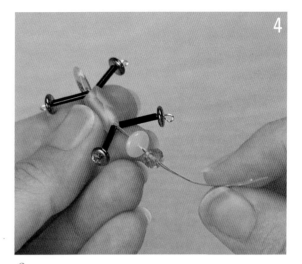

four · Pull the wire ends out of the other side of the body, and then thread them through one white donut bead and one amber glass bead.

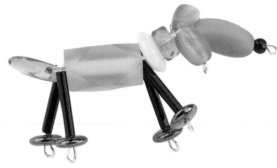

dog pin

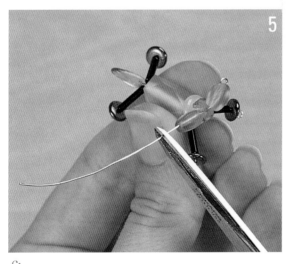

five · Separate the wires and string an oval bead onto each wire end. Trim one of the wires ¼" (6mm) above the bead, and then use round-nose pliers to loop the wire end. Repeat the process with the second wire to secure the other ear.

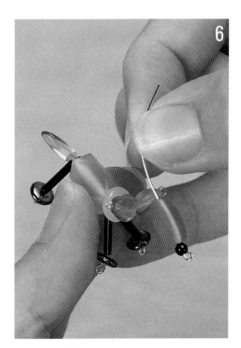

six · Loop one end of the 2" (5cm) wire. String a black seed nose followed by an oval bead onto the other end of the wire. Slide the beads down so they rest over the wire loop. Position the top of the head between the ears. To attach the head, wrap the remaining wire around the wires at the base of the ears. Glue the pin back to one side of the amber resin bead. Allow the glue to dry.

Follow the instructions on pages 102–103 to make a people pin. For the leash, loop a small length of wire around the person's hand and the dog's neck. To wear, secure both pins to your clothing.

home accents

use beads to add sparkle, whimsy and elegance to your living space. Whether you use just a few or a whole handful, crafting with beads can add impact and interest to common household items and transform them into beautiful home accents. You might already have stashed away in a drawer or closet what you need to create a brand new table set, vase, votive holder or decorative basket. Because you simply embellish, the process is both quick and rewarding.

With just a little forethought you can easily customize the projects to complement the décor of a specific room. Choose bead colors that match the walls and draperies so the finished piece blends into the room, or use bright contrasting colors to draw attention to your work.

A source of pride, these artfully unique beaded accents are sure to reward you with a sense of accomplishment for years to come.

CHAPTER

wire basket

MATERIALS

glass fruit beads (sold by the strand): pears, bananas and limes

glass leaf beads (sold by the strand)

wire basket, 8" (20cm) in diameter and 6" (15cm) tall

24-gauge black wire

wire cutters

This artful basket is a functional and beautiful addition to any home. The simple black wire base contrasts the brightly colored beads. Place the empty basket near a light source so the beads capture and color the light or fill the basket with bananas, oranges or pears to make a beautiful centerpiece.

one · Remove the fruit beads from the strand, if necessary. To ensure that the beads get equally distributed around the basket, organize them into groupings and set them in front of the basket sections. Cut the wire into several 24" (61cm) lengths.

*tip > If you have trouble locating a black wire basket you may choose to substitute a more accessible stainless steel basket. In which case, you'll need to use nontarnishing steel wire instead of black wire. This will insure that the wire will blend into the basket's construction and not detract from the beads. Don't limit yourself to fruit beads. Assorted pressed flower and leaf beads are widely available and make a beautiful blooming basket edge.

two · Wrap one end of a 24" (61cm) wire length one to two times onto the basket band. String the first bead of one grouping onto the open wire end. Slide the bead down the wire and hold the bead at the front of the basket. Wrap the wire around the band, and pull the wire tight. Continue stringing and wrapping until you reach the end of the wire. Wrap the wire end one and a half times around the basket band before trimming the excess wire.

three · Repeat step 2 until you've encircled the basket with beads.

bug plant stakes

MATERIALS

10mm art glass bead (for body)

disc-shape art glass beads (for thorax)

donut and round opaque glass beads (for head)

12" (30cm) of 24-gauge red wire (for wings)

14" (36cm) of 20-gauge wire (for stake)

round-nose pliers

These brightly colored bugs will surely attract attention as they bend and bob in your houseplants. The wire and heavyweight art glass beads are perfectly balanced so that the slightest movement will set the bumpy bugs in motion.

MORE SIMPLY
BEAUTIFUL
IDEAS

All the bugs are made the same way, just the colors and bead shapes change. The heavy art glass body beads counter balance the weight of the wire stake, head and thorax beads. If you need to substitute other bead varieties, look for similar-sized heavyweight beads.

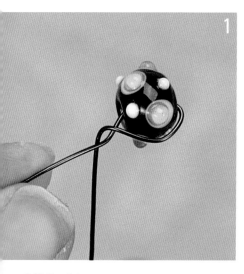

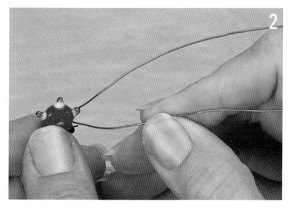

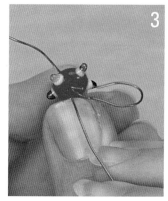

one · String one 10mm art glass bead (for the body) onto one end of the 20-gauge wire. Slide the bead 3½" (9cm) down from the end of the wire. Bend the wire end down against the side of the bead and twist it around itself under the bead.

two · Use the 24-gauge wire and a disc-shaped art glass bead to make the wings. Fold the end of the wire at a 90-degree angle. Thread the other end of the wire through the bead, and let the bead fall down so the bent wire end lays flat against the bottom of the bead. Loop the wire around the outside of the bead. Thread the wire end back up through the base of the bead and then pull the wire through the bead, leaving a wire loop wing ½" (1cm) long.

three · Loop the wire back around the bead to create a second wing. Thread the wire end back up through the base bead, creating a second wire loop wing ½" (1cm) long.

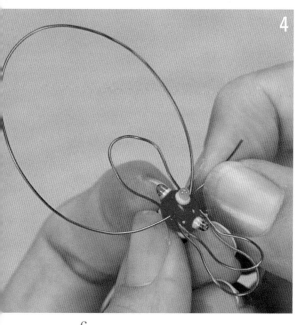

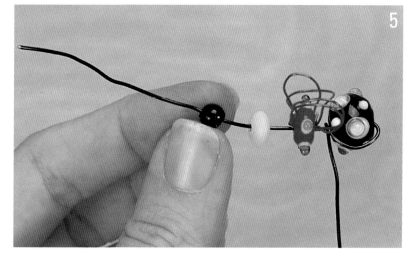

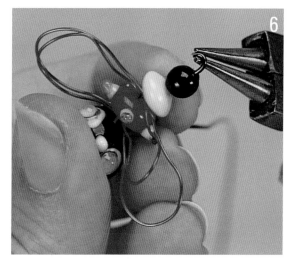

four · Repeat the process to make two more wings, for a total of four wings. Trim the wire ¼" (6mm) from the top of the bead, and then press the end flat against the top of the bead.

five · String the finished wing bead, one opaque glass donut bead, and one round opaque glass bead onto the short end of the 20-gauge wire.

six · Slide the beads down against the body bead. Trim the wire end. Using round-nose pliers, turn the end over (see "Looping Wire Ends," page 23).

wire-wrapped branches

MATERIALS

gold 6mm Miracle beads

light green 4mm Miracle beads

dry branches

28-gauge steel wire
(available at hardware stores)

This beautiful year-round centerpiece begins with natural branches that are tightly wrapped with inexpensive wire. The ends of each branch are budding with luminous miracle beads. The wire rotations and beads both capture and reflect light, drawing attention to the handiwork. The technique is simple, but plan to set aside some time—especially if you choose to wrap several branches.

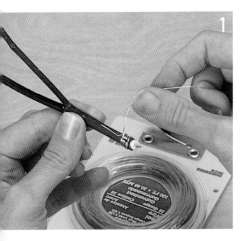

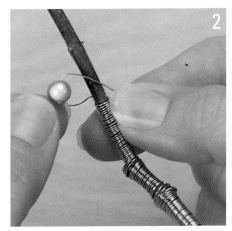

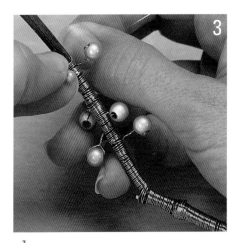

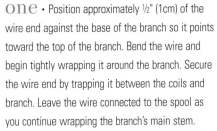

one · Position approximately ½" (1cm) of the wire end against the base of the branch so it points toward the top of the branch. Bend the wire and begin tightly wrapping it around the branch. Secure the wire end by trapping it between the coils and branch. Leave the wire connected to the spool as you continue wrapping the branch's main stem.

two · When the branch begins to narrow, unwind several feet of wire from the spool and cut the wire off the spool. String one 6mm gold bead onto the cut end, and slide the bead down the wire until it's 1" (3cm) from the branch. Fold the wire down toward the branch. Rotate the bead to twist the two wire parts together under the bead (see "Twisting Wire," page 23).

three · Continue wrapping the wire around the branch, stopping to string and twist more 6mm beads. Switch to 4mm light green beads when you reach the end of the branch.

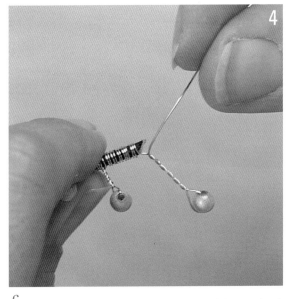

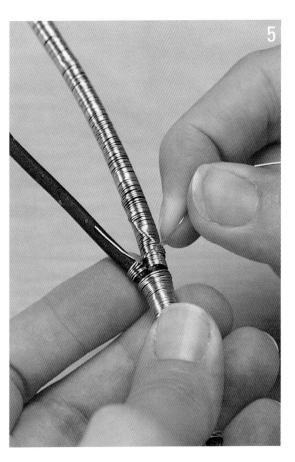

four · To end the branch tip, string one 4mm light green bead onto the wire and twist. Then wrap the wire end several more times around the branch tip before trimming the wire.

five · To begin wrapping a shoot, follow the instructions in step 1 to anchor a wire end where the branch forks. Wrap the wire around the branch until the branch narrows, then repeat steps 2, 3 and 4.

hanging votive candle holder

MATERIALS

four 6mm round silver beads

assorted glass beads

2¹⁄₂" x 2¹⁄₂" (6cm x 6cm)
glass votive candle holder

8" (20cm) square wire mesh
(I used WireForm Modeling WireMesh
with a ¹⁄₄" (6mm) diamond pattern)

votive candle

20-gauge nontarnishing silver wire

round-nose pliers

wire cutters

H ang a single votive candle from a large wall hook as a
room accent, or suspend a grouping of them at different
heights over a dining room table. For outdoor parties,
hang them from tree branches around the patio. Your guests
will be thrilled if you let them take one home as a party favor.

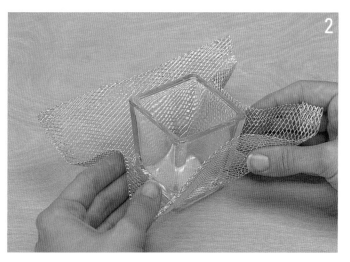

one · Fold over a ½" (1cm) edge on all four sides of the mesh to make a stronger and smoother top edge.

two · Place the votive candle holder in the center of the mesh square (folded side up) and bring each side of the mesh up against the glass. After shaping the mesh, slide out the glass and set it aside.

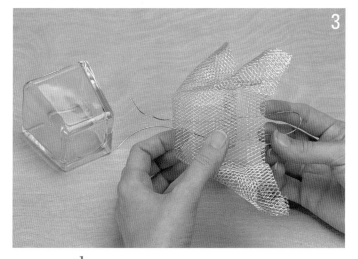

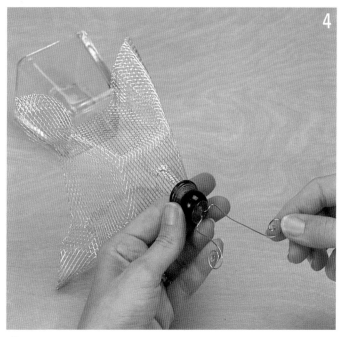

three · Fold one 14" (36cm) length of wire in half. Carefully hold the shaped mesh and thread both wire ends from the inside of the base to the outside. Gently pull the wire ends so that the center fold rests against the inside of the screen base and the ends hang below.

four · Bring the wires together and thread them through three glass beads. Separate the wires and bend them at an angle so they hold the beads up against the screen. Use round-nose pliers to begin spiralling one wire end (see "Spiralling Wire," page 24), then use your fingers to finish the shaping. Repeat the process to spiral the other wire.

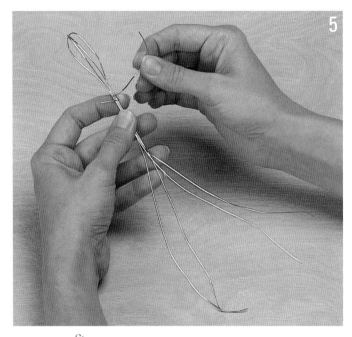

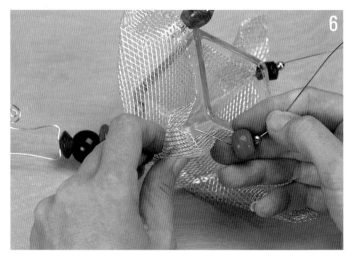

five · To begin assembly of the hanging system, fold two 21" (53cm) wire lengths in half together. Tightly wrap one 4" (10cm) piece of wire around all four wire lengths 2" (5cm) down from the fold (see "Wrapping Wire," page 24).

six · Place the glass into the shaped mesh. String one silver bead and one glass bead onto one of the four wires from the hanging system before threading the end of the wire through the two screen edges that come together to form a corner. Loop the wire end back up, and wrap it around itself before trimming the excess. Repeat this process for the other three wires at the other three mesh corners. It's important that each wire is of equal length so that the holder will hang level.

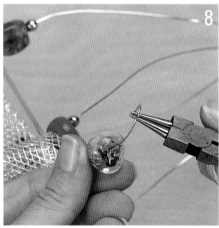

eight · Separate the wires to hold the bead in place. Bend the short end up under the bead, and then use round-nose pliers to spiral the long end. Repeat this process, begun in step 7, for the other three corners.

seven · Use one 5" (13cm) wire length to make the dangle for one corner of the shaped mesh. Fold the wire 3" (8cm) from the end. Hook one end through the mesh edge, and then thread both ends through one glass bead.

wineglass charms

MATERIALS

assorted glass beads
(translucent and opaque)

"E" beads

silver bell caps

stemware hoops (pick the size
that matches your glassware)

glass fruit charms: grapes,
oranges, raspberries, lemons

round-nose pliers

one • String the following onto
the open end of one hoop: one bell
cap, one "E" bead, one glass bead,
one glass charm, one glass bead, one
"E" bead, and one bell cap.

two • Use the round-nose pliers
to bend the wire end 90 degrees up
from the hoop. This will help prevent
the beads from sliding off, and it com-
pletes the clasp.

Place the finished charm around a
wineglass stem, threading the bent wire
through the manufactured loop. Unhook
the wire from the loop to remove the
charm before washing the stemware.

These elegant charms are a stylish
way to help your guests keep
track of their wineglasses. They
take only minutes to assemble and make
wonderful hostess gifts. Or make a
complete dining room set for your
home, matching the wineglass charms
to the beads on the Wire Basket (see
page 108).

MORE SIMPLY
BEAUTIFUL
IDEAS

I prefer lightweight glass charms for delicate stemware,
but if you have trouble locating them, look for more read-
ily available metal charms. Select a grouping of charms
in the same metal finish and pair them with glass and
spacer beads.

candle charm

MATERIALS

seed beads (a variety that will fit on the 1mm cord)

4mm silver metal beads

pressed-glass beads

eyelet phrases

candle

1mm clear stretch beading elastic (such as Stretch Magic)

8" (20cm) of 32-gauge steel wire

⅛" (3mm) eyelet setter and small hammer

round-nose pliers

clear tape

Personalize a candle or a bottle vase with a special message adorned with pressed-glass beads. The beaded charm is made with elastic so that it can be easily removed and reused. Birthday, anniversary and friendship eyelet messages can be found in the card-making section of craft stores.

ANOTHER SIMPLY BEAUTIFUL IDEA

This sparkling bottle charm is made exactly like the candle charm, although it uses less elastic. The bottle charm requires a slightly tighter fit so that it won't slide down the glass.

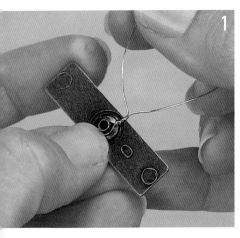

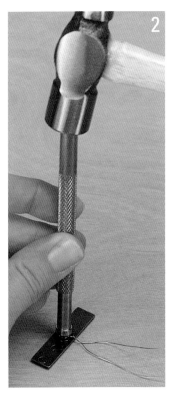

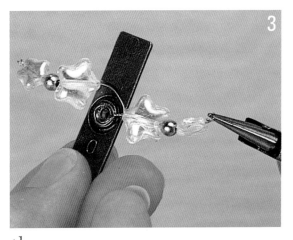

one · Loop and then twist the center of the wire around the metal back of the eyelet phrase.

two · Lay the eyelet phrase right side down on a protected work surface. Use an eyelet setter and a hammer to pound the metal backing flat over the wrapped wire.

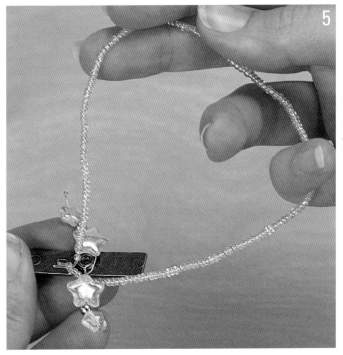

three · Separate the wires, and then string the following sequence onto each wire end: one pressed-glass bead, one silver metal bead and one pressed-glass bead. Trim the excess wire, and then loop each cut wire end with round-nose pliers (see "Looping Wire Ends," page 23).

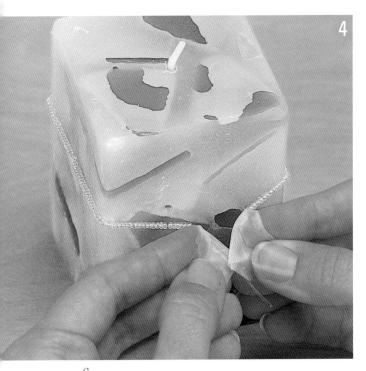

four · Cut a generous length of the elastic so it will comfortably wrap around the candle; include a couple extra inches for knotting. Tape one end of the elastic, and then string the length with seed beads. To ensure a snug fit, wrap the beaded elastic around the candle and then add or remove beads as necessary.

five · Tie the ends of the seed bead strand into an overhand knot (see "Tying an Overhand Knot," page 18). Loop the knotted section of elastic between the beaded wires and eyelet. Place the finished charm around the candle. Be sure to keep the beaded charm away from the candle flame, and remember to not leave a burning candle unattended.

nautical table set

MATERIALS

assorted glass beads, including some with sandwashed or slightly rough finishes

silver metal beads

silver charms: starfish, sea turtle, dolphin, clamshell, seahorse

four 2" (5cm) silver-finish eye pins (per ring)

fabric place mat

3¾" (10cm) cork coaster

19" (48cm) of size 1.8mm blue leather cord (length may vary depending on ring size)

18" (46cm) of size 1mm clear stretch beading elastic (such as Stretch Magic)

jewelry glue or Aleene's Platinum Bond Glass & Bead Slick Surfaces Adhesive

blue sewing thread

sewing needle

wire cutters

round-nose pliers

Perfect for someone who loves the ocean, this marine-inspired set combines silver charms, tumbled-glass beads and blue leather cord.

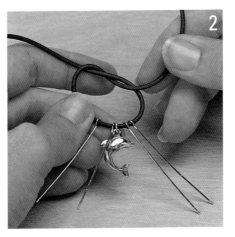

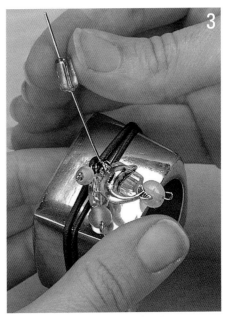

one • With a needle and thread, stitch a silver charm to each corner of the place mat. Sew on the underside of the mat to conceal your stitches and knots.

two • For the napkin ring, string the following onto one end of the leather cord: two eye pins, one charm and two eye pins. Trap the eye pins and charm in an overhand knot (see "Tying an Overhand Knot," page 18). Position the knotted eye pins in the center front of the napkin ring. Bring the leather cord ends together in the back of the ring, and then wrap the long end around the ring a second time. Tie the ends together in a square knot (see "Tying a Square Knot," page 18). Trim the cord ends and add glue to the overhand knot (in front) and the square knot (behind) to secure.

three • String one or two glass beads onto each eye pin. Trim each pin end below the beads, and then loop each wire end with round-nose pliers (see "Looping Wire Ends," page 23).

four • For the coaster, randomly string silver metal beads and glass beads onto 12¼" (31cm) of an 18" (46cm) length of stretch beading elastic. Bring both elastic ends together and tie them in an overhand knot. Stretch the beaded circle around the coaster's edge. Working your way around the coaster, pull the beads away from the cork, apply glue, and re-place the beads against the glue.

five • Apply a small bead of glue to the outside edge of the coaster, above the beads. Wrap the leather cord over the glue. Bring the cord ends together and begin to tie a square knot (see "Tying a Square Knot," page 18). String a charm onto one of the cord ends, and then finish tying the square knot.

wicker & flower table set

MATERIALS

assorted pressed-glass beads: flowers and leaves

copper seed beads

bronze leaf beads

4" x 4" (10cm x 10cm) wicker coasters

napkin rings

fabric place mat

19" (48cm) of size 2mm natural leather cord (length may vary depending on the size of the ring)

20-gauge wire

sewing thread (match place mat color)

sewing needle

jewelry or Aleene's Platinum Bond Glass & Bead Slick Surfaces Adhesive

wire cutters

round-nose pliers

Flower and leaf glass beads transform plain purchased linens, wicker napkin rings and coasters into garden-inspired accessories for the table.

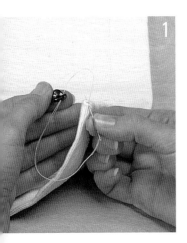

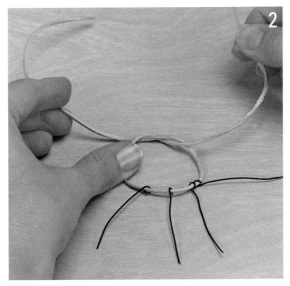

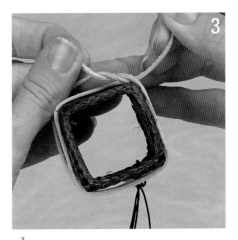

one · Use the needle and thread to stitch one bronze leaf bead to each corner of the place mat. Sew from the underside of the mat to conceal your stitches and knots.

two · For the napkin ring, use round-nose pliers to shape five 2" (5cm) lengths of 20-gauge wire into five eye pins. String the eye pins onto the leather cord, and then trap them in one overhand knot 7" (18cm) from one end (see "Tying an Overhand Knot," page 18).

three · Position the knotted eye pins in the center front of the napkin ring. Bring the leather cord ends together in the back of the ring, and then wrap the long end around a second time around the ring. Tie the ends together in a square knot (see "Tying a Square Knot," page 18). Trim the cord ends and add glue to the knot to secure.

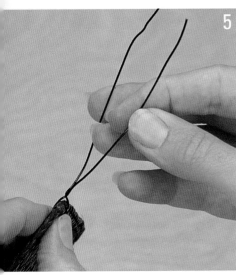

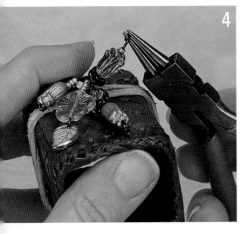

four · String a random combination of copper seed beads and pressed-glass flower and leaf beads onto each eye pin. Trim the pin end and loop each end with round-nose pliers (see "Looping Wire Ends," page 23).

five · For the coaster, thread one end of an 8" (20cm) length of wire through a corner opening in the wicker. Pull half the wire length through the

coaster to make two 4" (10cm) wires. Twist them together. Repeat the process to attach one wire to each of the remaining three corners.

six · String a random combination of two to three leaf beads, flower beads or copper seed beads onto each wire. Trim the wires with wire cutters and then use round-nose pliers to loop each end.

beaded flower decoration

MATERIALS

rainbow seed beads

Capri gold 6mm faceted crystal bead

24-gauge white wire: four 10" (25cm)
pieces (for the petals), 5¼" (13cm)
piece (to thread crystal), and 4" (10cm)
piece (to wrap petals to form flower)

round-nose pliers

B eautiful beaded flowers add elegance and sparkle to a wrapped gift. Wiring beads into flowers is an old tradition; I've updated and simplified the process so that your beading will quickly bloom.

ANOTHER SIMPLY BEAUTIFUL IDEA

This beaded flower makes the perfect embellishment for any glass ornament. To make a larger flower, increase both the wire lengths and number beads on each petal. To increase the fullness of the flower, add an additional three petal set. To make a smaller flower, decrease the number of beads on each flower petal and omit one of the three petal sets. Add clear mini marbles inside the glass ornament to complement the flower.

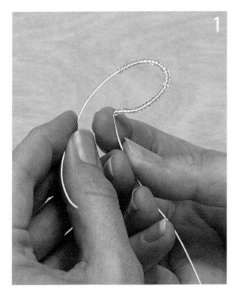

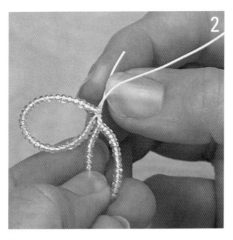

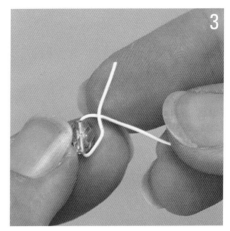

one · Begin making the first three-petal set with one 10" (25cm) length of wire. Bend the wire 4" (10cm) from the end and then string approximately thirty-six rainbow seed beads onto the wire. Loop the wire end back down against the first bead, and then twist the wires together once to trap the beads in the first petal loop.

two · String another thirty-six rainbow seed beads onto the wire, and then loop the wire back down to the base of the second petal. Rotate the petal once to twist the wires together. Repeat this step to make a third petal with the remaining wire end, completing one petal set. Repeat steps 1 and 2 to make three additional petal sets.

three · String a crystal bead onto the 5¼" (13cm) length of wire to make the flower stamen. Fold the wire down, and twist it under the bead.

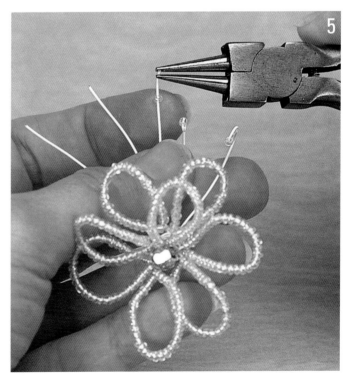

four · Center the beaded stamen between the four petal sets. Hold the five wire ends in one hand and tightly wrap the 4" (10cm) wire under the petals with the other hand (see "Wrapping Wire," page 24).

five · String one seed bead onto the end of each wire. Use round-nose pliers to loop each wire end so that the beads won't slide off (see "Looping Wire Ends," page 23).

resources

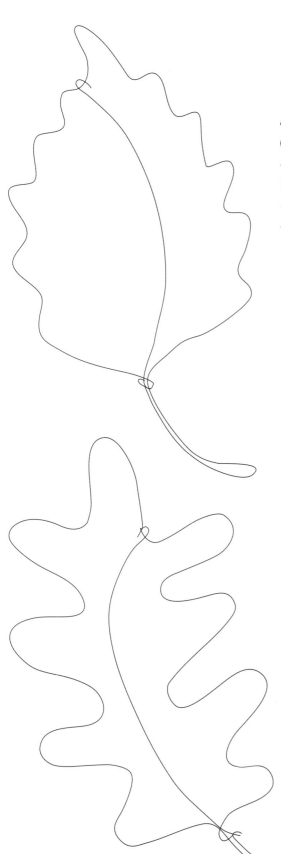

AMACO
(AMERICAN ART CLAY CO., INC.)
4717 West 16th Street
Indianapolis, IN 46222
(800) 374-1600
www.amaco.com
• *WireForm Modeling WireMesh*

BEADALON
(866) 423-2325
www.beadalon.com
• *beading wires and tools*

DUNCAN ENTERPRISES
5673 East Shields Avenue
Fresno, CA 93727
(800) 438-6226
www.duncancrafts.com
• *Aleene's Platinum Bond Glass & Bead
Slick Surfaces Adhesive*

FISKARS BRANDS, INC.
School Office & Craft
7811 W. Stewart Ave.
Wausau, WI 54401
(800) 500-4849
www.fiskars.com
• *Softouch Micro-Tip scissors*

G-S SUPPLIES
408 Saint Paul Street
P.O. Box 31091
Rochester, NY 14603-1091
(800) 295-3050
www.gssupplies.com
• *G-S Hypo Cement*

HALCRAFT, USA
30 West 24th Street
New York, NY 10010
(212) 376-1580
www.halcraft.com
• *tiny glass marbles*

SOFT FLEX COMPANY
P.O. Box 80
Sonoma, CA 95476
(707) 938-3539
www.softflexcompany.com
• *Soft Flex*

TONER PLASTICS
699 Silver Street
Agawam, MA 01001
(413) 789-1300
www.tonerplastics.com
• *Fun Wire*

WESTRIM CRAFTS
7855 Hayvenhurst Ave.
Van Nuys, CA 91406
(800) 727-2727
www.westrimcrafts.com
• *cords, findings, beads*

patterns for Wire Leaf Bookmarks, page 90

index

THE BEST IN CREATIVE INSTRUCTION AND INSPIRATION IS FROM NORTH LIGHT BOOKS!

• THESE BOOKS AND OTHER FINE NORTH LIGHT TITLES are available from your local art & craft retailer, bookstore, online supplier or by calling 1-800-448-0915.

NEW IDEAS IN RIBBONCRAFT

Create gorgeous home decor projects quickly and inexpensively with ribbons! Utilizing traditional, easy-to-follow techniques to create fresh, vibrant designs, Susan Niner Janes provides 25 exciting projects, including lampshades, towels and pillows, wedding keepsakes, baby blankets, purses, desk accessories and much more. A wide variety of styles and helpful templates—even no-sew projects on satin, felt, terry cloth and paper—make this book perfect for beginning and advanced crafters. ISBN 1-58180-351-6, paperback, 128 pages, #32323-K

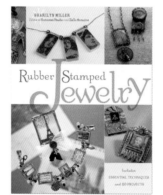

RUBBER STAMPED JEWELRY

Now you can combine the self-expressive qualities of rubber stamping with the elegance of jewelry-making. It's easier than you think! Sharilyn Miller provides all of the tips and techniques you need in 20 exciting wearable art projects. ISBN 1-58180-384-2, paperback, 128 pages, #32415-K

FAIRY CRAFTS

Explore a wondrous world of magic and imagination with Fairy Crafts! Inside you'll find 23 exciting projects that you and your children can make together. Each one features charming, easy-to-follow instructions that are guaranteed to get your little ones thinking creatively including poseable fairies, dress-up costumes, pretty flower invitations and beautiful keepsakes and gifts. You'll also find fun fairy stories to read together-stories that will engage the imagination and encourage your children to create their own enchanted adventures. ISBN 1-58180-430-X, paperback, 96 pages, #32594-K

WILD WITH A GLUE GUN

Designed to inspire friends to gather around a table, break out the projects and create with abandon, Wild with a Glue Gun offers a stunning array of craft projects, while showing craft clubs and other small groups how to foster an atmosphere of creative sharing. ISBN 1-58180-472-5, paperback, 144 pages, #32740-K